DECEMBER 6

DECEMBER 6

From the Montreal Massacre to Gun Control:
The Inside Story

Heidi Rathjen and Charles Montpetit

M&S

Canadian Cataloguing in Publication Data

Rathjen, Heidi
December 6 : from the Montreal massacre to gun control : the inside story

ISBN 0-7710-6125-0

1. Gun control – Canada.   2. Coalition for Gun Control.
3. Montréal École Polytechnique Women Students Massacre, Montréal, Quebec, 1989.   4. Rathjen, Heidi.   5. Cukier, Wendy.
I. Montpetit, Charles, 1958- .   II. Title.

HV7439.C3R37 1999   63.3'3'0971   C99-931627-3

We acknowledge the financial support of the Government of Canada through the Book Publishing Industry Development Program for our publishing activities. Canadä

We further acknowledge the support of the Canada Council for the Arts and the Ontario Arts Council for our publishing program.

Typeset in Minion by M&S, Toronto
Printed and bound in Canada

McClelland & Stewart Inc.
The Canadian Publishers
481 University Avenue
Toronto, Ontario
M5G 2E9

1 2 3 4 5   03 02 01 00 99

In memory of
Geneviève Bergeron
Hélène Colgan
Nathalie Croteau
Barbara Daigneault
Anne-Marie Edward
Maud Haviernick
Maryse Laganière
Maryse Leclair
Anne-Marie Lemay
Sonia Pelletier
Michèle Richard
Annie St-Arneault
Anne Turcotte
Barbara Klucznik Widajewicz
and all the others who are shot every year.

ACKNOWLEDGEMENTS

When we talk about this book as being both youth-oriented and for adults, we often get puzzled looks in return. Yet there is little to be surprised about. Instead of opting for academic detachment, we have written this story from a very subjective point of view – that of a student caught up in the whirlwind that started on December 6, 1989. Whether she's younger or older than you are, we feel that her tale will appeal to all ages.

This is why we'd like to start with a salute to the fifteen-to twenty-two-year-olds who made sure that the narrative was as accessible as possible. Thanks to Julie, Jasmine, Billie, Ariane, Kim, and Linda for their incisive comments, as well as the others who encouraged us throughout this effort.

As for the people who, over the years, supported the call for tougher gun control, a complete list of names would run into the thousands, so we hope we'll be forgiven for not going into details. Nevertheless, we must thank a few outstanding individuals who, for one reason or another, couldn't be fitted in the following pages. With heartfelt gratitude, here's to:

- Chantale and Steve, for holding the fort

- Antoine and Jim, for being our pillars of strength
- Subir, Jean, Yves, Stéphane, Martin, Jean-François, Michèle, and Noreen, for taking orders so cheerfully
- Lloyd, Keith, Mike, Graham, Steven, Liz, Peter, Lyne, Glenna, and David, for regional coordination
- Bob, Jim, Robert, Art, Dave, Norm, Tom, Brian, Vince, Pierre, and Fred, for police work extraordinaire
- Robert, Richard, Deborah, Ginette, Jean-Guy, Gilles, and Christiane, for assistance within the health network
- Steve, Robert, Alan, David, Françoise, Émile, Darryl, Jerry, and Matthew, for expertise on demand
- Leona, Judy, Arlene, Gael, Sandra, Virginia, Marilou, Mitzi, and Betty, for ensuring that women's voices were heard
- Dave, Philip, Claire, Patrick, Catherine, Barbara, and Anita, for first-class support
- Warren, Russell, Clifford, Dawn, Ian, Benoît, Guy, Pierrette, Joyce, and Mira, for daring to mix politics and principles, and to Eddie, Peter, Sheila, and Sue for helping them uphold those principles
- Peter and Jan, for wrestling those finances to the ground
- Clayton, for brilliant legal counselling
- and all our friends and families – especially Ian, Claudia, Yolaine, and Kathy – for bearing with us through it all.

YEAR ONE

"December 6, 1989 will remain one of the darkest pages of Montreal's history."

— Jean Doré, mayor of Montreal

I remember the start of it clearly: I was in a bad mood, and I didn't know why.

It's true, the Christmas-basket drive at the school had worn me down. It hadn't done well at first, so I had spent a good part of the week campaigning among the students, putting up signs and coming up with new ways to solicit donations. I had worked up a real sweat over this – but in the end the collection had turned out fine. I should have felt relieved.

Then again, like all the students at l'École Polytechnique, I was caught up in the end-of-term turmoil. During the previous weeks, everyone's workload had expanded beyond expectation; we had fallen behind in every subject and were frantically calculating how many hours were left to prepare for each exam. I was in my last year, and failing any one subject would mean I couldn't graduate in the spring. Sorting out canned goods had been a light respite from the pressure, but now that I was back in the graduating students' lounge, I had to get back to my term papers.

It was a little past five and there were few people around, most of them absorbed in their own notes. The last classes of the semester would be ending in less than half an hour. I had just pulled out my Hydraulics report when another student burst into the lounge.

"There's a guy with a gun out there."

He looked worried, but to me what he'd said didn't make sense. Why would there be a gunman in an engineering school? We stared at him without understanding, and he didn't argue with us. He went in a corner and sat down in silence.

Then the shots rang out.

They were barely recognizable – not the noise that you hear in the movies. They sounded like planks of wood hitting the floor, maybe, not *gunshots*.

Finally the student's warning sank in, and we slowly started to react, locking the door and turning off the lights. "Don't say a word! He might come this way!"

Everyone shut up. Two guys slid under the table with their knees up against their chins. Another student got a hold of the phone and called the police in hushed tones. I took the seat of a broken chair and held it in front of my chest, like a shield. I felt silly, because there was no way anyone would break in here and start shooting! I refused to think about what could happen next, but I thought I should do something to protect myself. . . .

And someone said – it might have been me, I'm not sure – "Hey! We could be on the news tonight!"

2

"The worst catastrophe to have happened to us since the last war."

    – Federal Opposition spokesperson Marcel Prud'homme

Forty-five minutes is a very long time to wait when you don't know what's going on.

We were all on edge, but we kept our heads. Whenever there was a knock on the door, we'd hesitate, make sure they were students, then quickly let them in and lock up again. There would be a brief exchange of whispers, but as soon as we realized that the newcomers didn't know any more than we did, we'd return to our this-can't-be-possible state.

There were many more gunshots, and screams too – there was a girl's voice, calling for help. One student got up, but another held her back.

"Are you insane? You can't go out there!"

"I want to see if I can do something."

"You can't! If he sees you, you could get shot yourself!"

"I'll take my chances. I can't stay here while –"

"Wait for the police, they've *got* to be on their way!"

"It may be too late by then. I'm going."

"No!"

She walked out before he could add another word, but she was only gone a minute. When she came back, she was completely out of breath.

"He's at the end of the corridor!"

"Did he see you?"

"Don't know. Could be."

"Don't you dare go out again!"

We'd have asked a lot more questions, but we had to keep quiet, so we didn't push for details.

And we waited. And waited. And waited.

You don't get bored in a situation like this – just terribly restless. Whenever we thought things had quieted down, another round of bullets would shatter the silence, smashing our hopes. The closer the gunshots got, the more we huddled, fearing the worst.

What are the police waiting for? How long does it take to see that this is an emergency?

I no longer dared to look at anyone, afraid that the dread in their eyes would confirm my own fears. I wanted to crawl inside my head, stop thinking, turn the page, and move on to other things. To the term projects I still had to hand in. To the parties where we would unwind from the fall semester.

It didn't stick. *Nothing* has any importance when one may only have a few more minutes to live – all options are put on hold, and the future loses all significance. I could barely imagine the shooter bursting into our room, and I certainly wasn't able to follow that scenario to its conclusion. Every second or so, I kept telling myself that everything would be all right, and I clung to that mantra with desperate hope.

Then there were no more gunshots – just silence. I kept expecting more blasts, but all I could make out were the clicks of the heating ducts and the whisper of the air vents. And then there were heavy footsteps, and baritone shouts in the distance. At long last, the cavalry had arrived.

᠀

By the time the police escorted us out, various rumours had already spread: the gunman had shot himself, an accomplice was still at large, hostages had been taken (these were the reasons why the police hadn't entered the school any sooner).

I was so relieved just to be in the open air. In spite of what we had gone through, none of it seemed as dreadful as it must have to everyone on the outside. I had heard the screams, I had seen the blood in the corridor – a trail of droplets, snaking towards the nearest staircase – but the horror hadn't struck me yet. I was numb, my emotions as paralyzed as my ability to think rationally.

The police told us to go home, but I lived in a small room in the student residence, and alone was the last thing I wanted to be. When my friend François invited me and some other students to his apartment a few blocks away, we jumped at the chance. We needed to stay together . . . and to find out more about what had happened.

When we turned on the TV, the shooting at our school was on every channel. We couldn't take our eyes off the screen.

It was much worse than we had imagined. As well as the journalists who were stationed at the school, reporters had been sent to the emergency wards, and their words were not reassuring:

". . . a large number of police officers are now on location. And ambulances keep arriving as we speak . . ."

". . . the wounded are said to have been found on both the second and third floor. At least two have already been taken to the hospital, but many more are being treated right here . . ."

". . . the Montreal General Hospital got most of the wounded. There are six of them, including a minor case, a young woman who already left with her parents. As for the others, four women and one man, they're in the operating room . . ."

". . . multiple wounds, to the chest, belly, and legs. A girl is currently undergoing plastic surgery . . ."

". . . the points of entry are very small, and the points of exit are very large, with massive destruction of tissues involved. The bullets virtually exploded inside the bodies . . ."

". . . it's possible some of them won't make it through the night . . ."

This wasn't right – it couldn't be. This was our school they were talking about, not casualties in a civil war!

When we learned that the intruder had started shooting in a fourth-year Mechanical Engineering class, it became even more troubling. *We* were mostly fourth-year students, and we knew some of the students in . . . Then I remembered, *Nathalie was in that class!*

Nathalie Provost was the first person I spoke to when I arrived at the school. We both became class reps at the same time, and we worked on so many projects together that I simply lost count. Her enthusiasm was the most infectious I'd ever come across, and I would have been hard-put to name a nicer friend.

I immediately grabbed the phone and called her place but all I got was the recording on her machine, her voice sounding as chipper as usual. I left a quick message asking if she was safe, but my heart grew heavier still.

On the news, the toll rose with each report. First there were ten, then twenty people who had been shot. Three of them were dead, then four, and maybe more. Even the reporters' choice of words grew wearier: in time, the story was upgraded from a "drama" to a "tragedy," and then to a "massacre."

When one journalist started to sum up the press conference that the police had improvised, we leaned forward.

". . . Armed with a semi-automatic rifle, the intruder entered the classroom and, after a warning shot, he forced the sixty-odd students to separate into two groups, the boys on one side and the girls on the other. He told the boys to file out, and as soon as the door closed, he opened fire on the girls."

This is impossible, it's all a big mistake. Any minute now, everything will get cleared up.

There was a short pause, and an officer came on to give the body count.

"The man was seen on three different floors. A woman was shot dead on the second floor, along with six others in the same classroom. Four more victims were found in a third-floor room, and three more in the main-floor cafeteria."

Any minute now . . . Please.

"The gunman killed fourteen people and wounded thirteen. The fourteen killed were all women."

3

"You're a bunch of feminists. I hate feminists!"
> – The killer, before he opened fire on the students

Outrage? Horror? Complete and utter disbelief?

I've tried many times to pin down how I reacted.

I was in shock, and that obliterated everything else. The news reports seemed artificial to me, as if they applied to another reality, not mine. When journalists reconstructed the killer's path, I couldn't recognize the places I went to every day. When they said he'd leapt from desktop to desktop, firing at terrified students who were cowering on the floor, I couldn't imagine that these were my fellow students. When we were shown stretchers being wheeled into emergency rooms, I couldn't bear to think that –

I couldn't believe it. I *refused* to believe it.

"It was a human hunt. We were the quarry."

"We thought it was a joke. If we had reacted faster, maybe we could have done something – he was right in the middle of the room. But after he fired, we just did what he ordered."

"Everyone ducked under their desks. I only had a bullet graze my temple, but one of my friends fell beside me, and she was whimpering in a pool of blood. I don't even know if she's alive."

"I was walking down the second-floor corridor when the guy came out. He fired, and next to me, two women went down. A bullet missed my foot by a centimetre. I ran."

"I was holed up in a corner with three friends. We were joined by a woman who was bleeding profusely; I saw another woman take a hit in the head. The man stopped shooting to reload his weapon, and I fled."

"I fell to the floor. The man took five or six steps past me – and then he saw me. He came back, he fired another round at me. And I didn't die. I kept waiting with my hands on my ears, fully aware that it was a very futile thing to do. . . ."

"I found two students lying on the ground, one of whom had been hit in the eye. . . . I started to speak to her and comfort her, saying, 'If you can hear me, squeeze my hand.' To my surprise, she did."

"We would have got engaged in March. We had bought some land in her hometown. That's where the house would be, we were making plans. . . . Now, all I've got left is her sweater. No matter how hard I squeeze it, she's not there any more."

Once it was confirmed that the killer had committed suicide, the urgency of the coverage gradually subsided. In the absence of new developments, the interviews became rarer and the regular programs gradually took back the air.

I had been so wrapped up in the news reports that I hadn't realized the importance of getting in touch with my parents. Like others, I had simply waited for a break in the coverage to call home. When I finally did, I was almost surprised to hear that they had been sick with worry, as if it was *obvious* that I wasn't in any danger!

As soon as I had hung up, François rose and excused himself. He was supposed to meet his lab partners to finalize a report, and he was already late. We all motioned him off: "Fine, go ahead, see you around."

When he and I later talked about that night, he told me that he was well on his way before the absurdity hit him. *People had died, and he was going to work on a lab report?*

I knew what he meant; I behaved the same way. When I left his apartment shortly after ten, I set out to pick up my books from my locker. I still had to study for my exams: they were all that my life was about!

The police, of course, had other priorities. They weren't letting anybody in, not even the students who had left their keys, coats, or wallets behind. I watched a few of them argue with the guards at the entrance, and gave up on the idea of getting my things when I realized I wouldn't stand a chance.

I couldn't believe it. We had *never* been refused access to the school, not at night, not on weekends, not even during the summer holidays. "Poly" was our second home, a place we could retreat to no matter what. And now, without any warning, it had been taken away from us, making us intruders on our own turf.

Something finally clicked, and the night got a little colder, a little darker. The entire school had become a crime scene. I couldn't shake my head, deplore the incident, and move on. My studies, my friends, my life would be turned upside down, thoroughly and for a long time.

I spent the rest of the evening around campus, drifting from group to group. It wasn't about feeling safe: I wanted to keep talking, to make noise, to hide from my thoughts. I had trouble coming up with things to say, but I was even more afraid of abandoning the comfort of numbers.

The ambulances had left deep tire tracks in the snow by the student entrance – an incongruous detail, since vehicles never usually got that close to the doors. The Christmas decorations down the hill seemed out of place, as if yellow police-line tapes had become the only acceptable ornaments. Nobody dared to speak in a loud voice, and every silence in the conversations underscored our helplessness.

I wound up with the acquaintances of the missing at the auditorium of the University of Montreal, which was just a short walk away, and together we waited for the victims' names to be announced.

They never were, not that night. Before the list was made public, the police had to have the bodies identified by immediate family members. During the makeshift information session, the dean could only tell us which of the students had

been sent to the hospital – and survived. There weren't that
many of them, but when Nathalie's name came up, I was
flooded with relief. She was *alive*, that was all I needed to
know!

Around me, however, there was only agony on so many
faces. For those who were still waiting for a name, the long
night was just beginning. . . .

4

"You can't take it and you can't accept it. When a kid goes to school until she's twenty-three, and her life ends in such a brutal fashion, the whole of society makes you want to vomit."

– Father of one of the victims

The media were back with a vengeance the next morning. When I woke up, a TV crew was already in the student lounge of my residence, and they were busily searching for engineering students.

I hung up on them when they phoned, but it didn't keep one producer from finding my room. When I opened my door, she made a very fast plea on behalf of her crew.

"No thanks," I repeated. "I don't want to be on TV, and I have nothing to say that you'd want to hear."

The few interviews I had witnessed so far had been very disturbing. Most of the students were as stunned as I was last night, and their lack of emotion meant that they didn't come across very well. I was afraid I'd sound like that, too.

"But we're told you were at the school when the killings took place. As a woman in a male-dominated field, couldn't you tell us how you feel about . . ."

I must have winced. That was one thing that I particularly disliked about the media coverage. Just because there were few women in engineering, reporters were assuming that a pattern of sexism was pervasive in our school, and that it was somehow linked to the massacre.

"Sorry, but no. You're implying that female students are either unwelcome or mistreated at Polytechnique. It's simply not true: the entire student community would like the number of women to go up, and the teachers treat everyone the same. If there's one place where female engineers are considered *normal*, this is it! And now, our teachers are being forced to defend themselves against accusations that were never even an issue!"

"Perfect!"

"Excuse me?"

"That's a great statement, and a very important one. You're the only person who has made that point so far; it would be a pity to let it go unsaid. Couldn't you repeat it with the cameras rolling?"

"Well . . ."

"You don't have to come downstairs if you don't want to. I can bring the crew here, no hassle. . . ."

What could I have replied? As upset and camera-shy as I was, I did want to defend my second family. I gave in, and I'm glad I did. I got a lot of positive feedback, most of it along the lines of, "Thank you, thank you, thank you for what you said!"

Coincidentally, as soon as the camera crew left I got a call from Alain Perreault, the president of the Polytechnique student association. He was swamped with media inquiries, and since I had been on the executive council in the past, he wondered if I would be prepared to get involved again – this time as a spokesperson. Sharing the workload wasn't his only motive. Except for one student who had gone home, the council was all male that year (as opposed to the previous year, during which women had been a majority). Given the nature of the crisis, a female representative was a must.

There was no need to ask me twice. I felt lost, distraught, restless: Alain's offer would be the best of therapies. It wouldn't just keep me busy; helping out would make me feel useful . . . and less vulnerable.

It would also cause me to miss the event I most wanted to attend: a massive vigil was scheduled for later on, and I couldn't wait to join the crowd and be swept up by the atmosphere. My guts were still balled up in a tight knot, and I desperately needed to cry my eyes out.

But first, Alain and I were to meet Prime Minister Brian Mulroney and his wife Mila, who wanted to offer their condolences to school representatives. Their flight, however, was delayed because of bad weather.

When darkness fell on the campus, we were still waiting in the corridor, chewing on our frustrations. Outside, polar temperatures and stinging winds didn't prevent thousands of people from assembling in front of the school. The mourners lit candles in memory of the victims and solemnly pushed roses into the snowbanks. The crowd then slowly filed onto the street for a silent procession, and we were left behind with our pent-up emotions.

By the time the prime minister's limousine finally showed up, it had become very hard for us to see the meeting as anything but staged, awkward, and phony.

The dignitaries were as nice as they could be, but nobody knew what to say. After all, the prime minister didn't know anything about us, and he certainly couldn't make us feel any better. So the conversation went "This is so terrible" and "My deepest sympathies," with long awkward silences and everyone trying to express more sentiment than was possible in such a stale context.

It was a political gesture, nothing more.

⁂

Visiting Nathalie was terribly disconcerting. It was my friends and I who walked in with sad faces, terrified at the idea of saying something wrong, and *she* was the one who tried to cheer us up. Confined to her hospital bed, she did everything she could to convince us that she was all right – a daunting performance, given all the visitors who were lining up to see her. A good twenty people were already waiting when we got there, some of whom had just arrived from Quebec City.

By this time, the media had already made her into some kind of icon: of all the people who had faced the killer, she was the only one who had tried to reason with him.

"We're just women who are studying engineering," she had told him, "not necessarily feminists. . . . Just girls who want to lead a normal life."

For her trouble, she had been hit three times. As if in slow motion, she had seen the light go out in many of her class-mates' eyes and then she found herself falling, a wave of heat spreading through her entire body.

She had been hit in the temple, leg, and foot. Miraculously, none of the bullets had struck a bone, so they hadn't exploded – the burns from each shot would leave more of a scar than the wounds themselves. Remarkably lucid, she seemed less concerned about her well-being than con-fronting the reporters who were badgering the hospital per-sonnel for an interview with a survivor.

"I want all the girls who were considering a career in engi-neering to keep at it, no matter what happened," she said, still lying in bed, during a press conference that very afternoon. "Please, we women have to stick together. . . . We cannot let this tragedy get to us.

"Also, there are guys who are feeling very bad about what happened. They keep thinking that they were guilty of some-thing, and it's not true. There is only one criminal in all of this, and he's already dead. Everybody else did everything they could."

A girl defending the *guys*? Many people had trouble under-standing that one: in the media and on the street, there were plenty of ignorant people who blamed the male students for not having protected their classmates. With comfortable hindsight, anyone could rewrite the scene and have the guys overpower the attacker.

But the truth is, it was perfectly normal to have felt help-less in this situation. Without any precedent to draw on, the students couldn't have understood what was going on, much less imagine what would happen once they left the classroom. All that could be said about their accusers is that *they weren't there* – and that they watched too much TV.

Unfortunately, her message couldn't prevent one male student from taking his own life, an additional tragedy which, in turn, pushed both of his parents to suicide. Still, Nathalie's words must have comforted thousands of others – she later received hundreds of letters to that effect. But I was startled by the number of people who only retained that she had "denied" being a feminist. Like most survivors hounded by reporters, she soon came to loathe the media, and the feeling only got worse when the depression that she thought she had initially avoided crept up on her during the following months.

At least she did survive. When the list of the deceased was finally made public, I was horrified to recognize the names of other girls I knew.

It was an unexpected shock, as harsh as the one I experienced while under siege. Although the victims were never just numbers to me, I had been in such denial that their death only became completely real as of that point. There was Anne-Marie Lemay, a sweet and cheerful girl, whom I'd just helped organize the yearbook pictures. There was Barbara Daigneault, my friend Eric's girlfriend, who was following in the footsteps of her father, a teacher at the École de technologie supérieure. . . . These were beautiful, caring, hardworking, energetic girls . . . and I realized that these memories were all that was left of them.

I called a childhood friend and I cried with her for a good half-hour.

Still, I got off easy by comparison. I wasn't injured, hadn't witnessed any killing, and didn't feel traumatized. I may have had trouble sleeping, felt constant shivers and, for a long time, been unable to eat a full meal, even when I was hungry. But as long as I had work to keep me busy, at least I could function – and that's what saved me. I cannot imagine how I would have coped had I also been forced to rest.

In conjunction with the student association, I had flowers sent to all the survivors and made sure that all those who were up to it got a few visitors. After such an outpouring of raw hatred, they must have been starved for affection, and we figured we should provide them with a minimum of companionship.

We didn't know any of them intimately, except for Nathalie, and the occasion didn't exactly lend itself to conversations about the weather. Or studies. Or holidays. Or the murders. What was left – "We are here to provide a minimum of companionship"? I had never encountered anyone who'd had a brush with death before, and I felt so intimidated that I didn't even dare to ask about their injuries!

We weren't very good at this kind of thing, but visiting them at least allowed us to see that all the damage was under control; wounds were disinfected, sutured, and bound, which went a long way to reassure *us*. Then, after one of the patients asked if we could get him a new school jacket (the one he was wearing had had to be cut off), and another girl thanked us profusely for being her very first visitors (her family lived in

country), our feelings of incompetence gradually
l. We were all on the same team, and that was enough
to build a genuine connection.

Strangely, it was the seating arrangements for the collec-
tive funeral at Notre-Dame Basilica that sapped most of my
energy. The logistics were unbelievably complex, with the
seating priority ranging from personal friends to engineering
students to students at large, then on to the general public.
We had to create several waiting lists, and by the time the ceremony started, my team and I were still handing out last-
minute passes at a little windswept table on the church steps.
When we finally got inside, we had missed most of the
speeches from the school representatives.

As for the mass itself, I'm sorry to say I couldn't swallow any
of it – and I wasn't the only one, as a flurry of letters to the
editors would show. After the terrible ordeal, all of us women
needed to be reassured, to feel supported, to be told that such
hatred had no place in our society. As one of the last bastions
of masculinity, the Catholic Church could have scored major
points had it recognized its own excesses through the ages
and embraced us, even if just for a brief moment.

I can dream, can't I?

But they didn't say one word about the victims, what they
had accomplished, how they had died, or about their being
women. In the aftermath of the shootings, I found it especially offensive to see three dozen men in robes imploring
God's forgiveness for *our* sins, and lecturing us about the
almighty Father, Son, and Holy Spirit. Instead of letting the
grief flow from our hearts, all we got was tinkling bells,

clouds of incense, and morose music through and through.

Sitting in full view up in the front rostrum and grinding my teeth, I tried to take part in as little of the ritual as I could without looking disrespectful. The priests only read the names of the victims once, and they badly mispronounced one of them. Was this any way to bid farewell to fourteen women killed in the prime of their lives?

That afternoon, I attended the private ceremony organized by Anne-Marie's family in a tiny suburban church, and the contrast with the group funeral couldn't have been more marked. No gloomy shadows, no dreary organ, but bright lights and Anne-Marie's favourite songs from the days she sang in the church choir. Above all, the whole service was about *her*, the absurdity of the tragedy, and everyone's need for comfort. "You may or may not be religious," the priest said, "but turning to spirituality can help you get through this, if that's what you choose to do." We all hugged in the parking lot afterwards, completely drained, but our emotions in harmony. It was a much more genuine goodbye, most respectful for everyone involved.

(The sight of the coffin gave me a hard time, however. It was difficult for me to accept that my friend was now shut inside, forever stilled. Funeral parlours and chapels of rest get to me that way, and I always try to linger as little as possible – the irony of which would become plain a few months later, when I'd be looking for someone to sponsor my efforts.)

All through the first days, anonymous donors placed flowers in the snow by the main door of the school, and thousands of letters, telegrams, and faxes were piling up faster than we could acknowledge them. At first, we didn't know what to do with them all, but since they provided an outlet for everyone's grief, we decided to exhibit them as best we could. Both students and faculty, we hoped, would draw strength from the support.

There were too many items for any one bulletin board, so our dean, Roland Doré, let us use the study area on the sixth floor of the school. Open, spacious and well-lit, with large bay windows, it was just the right place for paying our respects.

"Go ahead, paste, staple, and hammer away," he said to me. "If need be, we'll re-plaster later." That was very good of him, for we thoroughly ruined the finish on all the walls: once in place, the cards, the drawings, the poems, and the banners covered every square centimetre, from floor to ceiling. The Montreal Botanical Gardens even let us borrow the plants that had decorated the chapels before the funerals.

I quickly realized that our tribute wouldn't be complete without pictures of the victims, so I contacted each family and asked if they could spare any. I had them framed, and mounted in custom-made exhibition cases. I felt terrible for making all these requests – I thought I was imposing on both the school and the parents at a time when they had bigger worries. But far from being treated as a nuisance, I found I was a comfort to them. The administrators were well aware that these things had to be done, so they didn't cringe when I sent them the bills. And the family members knew how much the school had meant to their daughters and sisters, so they were glad to see that their classmates cared too.

Nevertheless, I hesitated a long time before showing them the result. The memorial was incredibly potent, and I wasn't sure they would find it easy to take in, especially when their daughters had been murdered just a few steps away.

Indeed, the experience would have been particularly trying for one of the fathers. A police officer, he had been among the first people to enter the school after the shooting, and he had endured the worst possible nightmare that he could have faced in the line of duty: when he walked into the classroom where the killer had committed suicide, he had recognized his own daughter amongst the bodies on the floor. In no uncertain terms, he told me he never wanted to set foot in the school again, and I feared every other parent would follow suit.

I shouldn't have worried – as understandable as his reaction was, he ended up being the only one who felt that way. When one couple brought in a photo album of their daughter for the memorial, they told me how much they appreciated what we had done, and this led me to overcome my fears. One evening when student activities were at their lowest, I took it upon myself to order a modest buffet, and I invited all the families to meet each other for the first time, far from the cameras and prying eyes.

Everyone was truly touched. The intensity of the testimonials and the comfort that they offered were a welcome respite from the turmoil that they endured, and sharing their emotions with people who knew exactly what they were going through must have done them a lot of good. Many even insisted on preserving some of the artwork that had been sent to us.

So soon after the tragedy, their courage and resilience were truly heartwarming. My having so much in common with the victims may even have led us to a special relationship, as if I could fill a small part of the void that their daughters had left behind. Whenever I was with them, I'd make an effort to be on my best behaviour, trying to earn their praise and longing for their approval. Much more than reason and ideals, their support gave true meaning to my actions.

That night, I understood how deeply they needed us to remember their daughters. We couldn't bring the girls back, but a lot could still be done on their behalf. . . .

5

"There is nothing we can do."

– Pierre Foglia, columnist for *La Presse*

First mourn, then work for change, said one poster after the tragedy.

No one disagreed with that. But no two people had the same idea of "change," or what kind of "work" would bring it about.

Putting a name on the killer hadn't been easy: he had shot himself in the face and hadn't been carrying any ID. The police investigated every gun store in the metropolitan area on the chance that he'd bought his semi-automatic weapon in one of them. He had, and the store's records led them to his name and apartment, but not to an explanation behind his outburst.

Marc Lépine didn't drink or do drugs. He was two courses short of being admitted to Poly. He hadn't been violent with the girls he had hung around with. However, he did express his frustrations in a letter that was found in his pocket. It said that he had tried to enrol in the army, but was turned down because of his "antisocial" behaviour. He believed that his life had been "ruined." And without going into details, he blamed feminists for his personal failures, angrily ending with a list of prominent women who would have been his next targets.

That was it. There was no mention of a sudden crisis that had pushed him over the edge. He'd been just a seemingly ordinary man whose feelings of inadequacies had suddenly taken over, prompting the rest of us to wonder how such tragedies could be avoided.

Many people chose to see what he did as the isolated act of an insane man. This didn't let anyone work for improvements – by their very nature, acts of madness are nearly impossible to predict. To accept this attitude would have meant that we had no way to fight back.

The war of the sexes sparked a lot of debates, in part because many commentators initially denied the nature of the crime. When women's groups called it an extreme case of violence against women, they were often accused of appropriating the event by the very papers that had sought their opinions. "Nothing proves that this imbalance is a sign of a greater social problem," a *Soleil* editorialist would write.

"It could have been fourteen blacks, even fourteen janitors!" argued a friend of mine, who didn't see any calculated motive in the shootings. Even those who recognized the killer's misogyny didn't necessarily concede that his attitude was a product of his environment. We had many passionate discussions on the subject, with the guys often on the defensive. Since in our small universe, we had all but banished such problems, even the most progressive among them had trouble understanding that discrimination was still a reality for many women, while others saw an irreducible link with sexism in society. "The massacre was the brutal culmination of a season of hatred," asserted the *Globe and Mail*. "It took the slaughter of fourteen women to focus attention on an escalating problem."

The violence also generated much controversy, with many people arguing that the massacre followed a pattern that had become banalized over the last few years. In routine succession, television, movies, and sensationalist news programs were put to blame, along with dozens of other factors, such as the increase in society's permissive attitudes, the way parents raise their children, the unemployment crisis, the stresses caused by poverty, the popularity of war toys, rock/punk/rap music. . . .

We also got long, rambling letters about international conspiracies, hallucinogenic experiences, and religious extremism. Animal-rights militants even asked us to forward their literature to the parents of the victims!

We didn't prevent anyone from focusing on these issues, but practical solutions were still hard to come by. We were mostly stuck with general conclusions like "we must build a better society based on peace and mutual respect," to reprise the words of the bishop of Valleyfield. Always a noble goal, but too vague for future engineers like us, who specialize in solving precise technical problems.

The killer's message wouldn't be heeded, that much was obvious – in the year after the shooting, the number of female students registering at Poly reached an all-time record. The student association also supported a number of meaningful campaigns – such as free self-defence seminars for underprivileged women – but most of all, we wanted to do something that would prevent a similar tragedy.

Yet there was one decisive factor that could be phrased in terms of nuts and bolts. It didn't address most of what had led to the massacre – no measure could – but it did address one key element:

Could the killer have inflicted as much damage without a high-powered semi-automatic weapon?

*

Concerns regarding these types of guns weren't new. For years, the country's chiefs of police had been asking the federal government to ban assault weapons. The massacre merely underscored the lack of political action to do so – and made the public notice how lax our current laws were.

Like most Canadians, I hadn't known how easy it was to get a gun. All anyone had to do was pay ten dollars for a Firearm Acquisition Certificate. If they were sixteen or older, had no criminal record, and checked the box attesting that they didn't suffer from a mental illness, they were entitled to as many rifles and shotguns as they wanted. (Handguns require an additional permit.)

According to the police, the Ruger Mini-14 used by the aggressor was one of the most dangerous long guns on the market. Some merchants refused to sell it, arguing it was a "killer's gun" that no self-respecting hunter would use. Having such firearms removed from circulation seemed like a sensible goal.

Just a few days after the shooting, a group of students, teachers, and other school personnel had come up with the idea of a petition. The media gave it positive coverage, and it caught on like wildfire.

PETITION

The undersigned call upon the authorities for the immediate enactment of laws forbidding anyone in Canadian territory from having in their possession any military or paramilitary weapon, with the exception of members of the Armed Forces and law-enforcement officers for the purpose of their duties.

I lost sight of it for a while – the memorial and other tasks took every moment of my time. But this changed when I became a delegate to the Congress of Canadian Engineering Students, which took place in early January, a week before the start of the new semester.

❧

To the uninitiated, a congress of student engineers might sound boring and tedious, but there are so many parties, outings, and workshops, it's more like an intense vacation, and I wouldn't have missed it for the world. Its purpose is to show students how to organize unusual fundraisers, set up

engineering camps for kids, and handle controversial issues –
all from the student perspective, based on real-life experiences. The atmosphere is convivial, and lasting friendships
are forged. It's also a great opportunity to set up a network
for a project like ours.

Alain discussed the petition with the congress organizers,
who all agreed to bring the petition to the congress floor to
be endorsed. They expected support to be unanimous, so
they scheduled only a short time for a debate on the proposal.

Big mistake. No one realized that some of the students
would be avid hunters or target shooters – just the kind of
people who might feel threatened by tougher gun laws. There
was a debate, and it was very protracted.

Advocates of gun control are often accused of giving in to
their emotions, but gun owners could be just as emotional . . .
only not about the same things. Aside from cars, few objects
claim as much allegiance from their users as weaponry. The
discussion heated up quickly, with catchphrases flying in
every direction:

"If people want to kill, they'll always find a way, guns or no
guns!"

"That's no reason to treat machine guns like baseball bats.
There's a huge difference between the two!"

"Hey, wait a minute, we live in a free country. As long as I
don't misuse my guns, no one should treat me like a potential
criminal!"

"You're defending a hobby in a shooting club. We're
talking about measures that would save lives!"

"So am I. If I'm the one who's attacked, my gun could save my life!"

"Not if your assailants have their own. With the advantage of surprise, just see who'll shoot first!"

"But if we ban guns, only criminals will have them!"

"Even that would be an improvement over fearing *everyone!*"

"If the Poly students had been armed, they might have stopped the killer in his tracks!"

"If the students walked around with guns, there would have been many more tragedies *before* he ever came along!"

It wasn't the first time these arguments were made, and they would keep surfacing for years to come. We were just entering the gun-control battle, but the rhetoric was universal.

One thing was clear, though: as brash as our opponents were, they weren't as numerous as those who agreed with us. If the organizers hadn't insisted that a unanimous decision was important, the great majority would have endorsed the petition, and the dispute would have ended there. Instead, the motion was postponed.

My heart sank. There was only one day left before we all went home, and the agenda was already overloaded.

Potential obstacles should have been ironed out *before* the issue was put to the crowd. You should never wait until there are hundreds of people in the room to put forward such an unconventional proposal.

I hadn't entered the discussion yet – I didn't feel confident enough to speak in front of so many people. But one by one, in the hallways, Alain and I talked to the dissenting delegates, trying to persuade them to change their minds, explaining that they were supposed to speak for their student associations, not just for themselves. Given that, out of the entire congress, so few were entrenched in their belief, could they truly say that they reflected the majority opinion on their campuses?

Our school team chipped away at the opposition into the night, but all our efforts weren't enough. When the debate resumed the next morning, two or three delegates hadn't budged at all. The motion wouldn't be unanimous.

Oh, what the heck, I thought. I'm shy and nervous and inarticulate in front of a crowd, but after having been so heavily involved in the aftermath of the shootings, I knew I had acquired a certain credibility, and now I felt I had to speak. I scribbled a couple of thoughts on a sheet of paper, and tried to block out of my mind how foolish I might sound.

It was only after I managed to get to a mike that I realized that I would be the last speaker. I swallowed hard, summoned my courage and dove straight in:

"Uh . . . My name is Heidi Rathjen, and I'm from l'École Polytechnique. By now you've probably heard all the arguments about gun control, but I think I might have something else to add. . . .

"I've talked to the victims' parents. They don't want anyone to forget what happened to their daughters, and they desperately wish some lasting good could come out of it. Increasing gun control is one way to do this – by making our society safer.

"Unanimous consent may not be significant to you, but without it, today's gesture has little impact. What we're asking is not exceptional, either: this congress has done it many other times, and we weren't even dealing with life-or-death matters that most students agree on. Now that this is indeed the case, it should be easier still to set our differences aside.

"If you oppose the petition for personal reasons, your refusal won't prevent the project from going forward: enormous support is coming in from everywhere, and we're not about to give up. But how will it look to the media, to the public, to the students back home if we, the people most closely affected by this, can't even agree on a simple thing like this?

"Some of you say this isn't your concern. But you're wrong. Engineering students were the targets here, and every campus will remain as vulnerable as ours was if nothing is done. Tomorrow, it could be your school a gunman shows up in."

Even as I spoke, I was startled to see how long I kept going. My voice was cracking near the end, but I managed to finish without falling to pieces.

"Take a stand for what is in our common interest. Your solidarity is of crucial importance."

There was a moment of silence. Then someone started clapping, and there was deafening applause for several minutes.

Some called it a "turning speech." For all intents and purposes, the vote that followed was unanimous: the opponents abstained, the petition was endorsed and, at the final banquet,

I was formally handed all the signatures that had been collected throughout the week. Alain immediately asked me to
take charge of the petition from then on, and I was asked to
give another speech!

It took me by surprise – I hadn't planned on getting so
involved. But given the circumstances, I couldn't possibly
have walked away.

6

"We can't legislate against this happening . . . You can't legis-
late against insanity."

> – Doug Lewis, federal minister of
> justice at the time of the killing

It hit me after the congress. I was way behind in my school-
work.

I hadn't taken any of the previous semester's exams. I
hadn't even opened a book since the day of the massacre.
Make-up exams would be offered to everyone in the coming
days, but I already knew I wouldn't be able to catch up.

I had no regrets. I would have taken on the petition project
no matter what.

It worked out all right. Special exemptions were granted to
the half-dozen of us who had helped in the immediate aftermath of the killings. I was told I could take two exams of my
choice, and the other courses would be graded according to
my earlier performances.

This was fine, except that handling the petition had prac-
tically become a full-time job. But I did get a makeshift office
at the back of the student conference room, plus a small

expense account and lots of volunteers – students who, like me, wanted to do *something*.

(One might have expected the scars of the tragedy to be all over the place when classes reconvened in mid-January. The wonderful exuberance that we were known for might have been tainted by dark undercurrents, and the school might have been marked for a very long time. But expecting that would have been a mistake. From the instant I walked back in, the familiar hustle and bustle surrounded me with reassuring energy. The hallways were packed, the conversations intense, the café's music loud and vibrant – everything we needed to rekindle our student life was in place. But one thing did change. Our eyes met more often, and we were much more courteous to each other – it was our subtle way of demonstrating our solidarity.)

Much had already been accomplished. The school had mailed the first fifty thousand petitions to all the companies in the database of the school's employment service. A lot of other organizations, banks, and unions were already calling for copies. Later, a famous Quebec artist, Pierre-Yves Pelletier, donated a design for a poster to enhance our campaign.

The students took care of the footwork. From the large oval table in the conference room, we sorted the messages of sympathy out from the signed petitions and the requests for information, we found new distribution outlets, and we sent out petition forms with cover letters encouraging everyone to duplicate the forms and spread the word.

With the steady stream of phone calls that were coming in, I hardly had time to handle the media inquiries, let alone

answer all the requests for more petitions. I was so overwhelmed, I couldn't see beyond the chaos. That is, until I
heard from Wendy.

≈

Wendy

When my sister came to visit me in Toronto, the first thing
she said upon bringing in the morning paper was: "Did
you hear someone shot fourteen women in Quebec?"

She must have read wrong, I thought. Maybe fourteen
people were wounded, or maybe it's the total for the last
month. I couldn't accept that such a mass killing had
occurred in my country. It felt like one of those reports
from far, far away, not an item from a nearby city.

Once I saw that she had it right, I spent the day in a state
of disconnection. I attended a big meeting with my administrators at Ryerson University, and I kept asking myself why
everybody was acting so normal. The world had changed:
for months afterward, I'd teach my courses thinking that it
could happen here, and I'd look at my daughter Sarah, won-
dering what if it had been her? To this day, my strongest
link has been not with the victims, but their parents.

My most powerful emotion, however, was anger.

I wasn't politically active. I didn't know who my MP
was, and the only protest I'd ever attended was a peace
rally that a friend had dragged me to. But I had worked for
the Ministry of Transportation, and I knew about road
fatalities and the measures that reduced them. When the

journalists who covered the massacre pointed out that nothing like this was being done about gun deaths, the comparison jolted me into asking, Why not?

I tried to join a group in favour of gun control, and found that none existed. Yet the experts who were being interviewed in the papers already seemed to agree on the measures that should be put in place to limit access to weapons. All that was missing was a little support.

So I made a few calls, enlisted board members, and founded Canadians for Gun Control, an organization that would push for stronger gun laws. If I could promote the purchase of teleconferencing equipment as a freelance consultant, surely I could do something about a cause that meant much more to me.

❧

Wendy's first letter stood out like a beacon amidst all the mail that I sorted in the students' conference room. Instead of going on at length about how sorry she felt for us, she was concise, constructive, and most optimistic about the outcome of our initiative.

To: Heidi Rathjen
Re: Gun Control
Enclosed is a copy of a recent letter sent to the Ontario Provincial Police Association and my rough translation of your original petition. If the Toronto newspapers won't print your petition for free, I may be able to persuade the

OPPA to pay for it. I added a column for addresses in some
of the copies that I am circulating, in case you want to do
follow-up with interested individuals.

Have you formally established a non-profit association,
which would allow you to accept donations, collect membership fees, etc.? Have you worked out an organizational
structure? Do you need help in doing this or would you
prefer to remain informal?

I also have a couple of suggestions for you to consider . . .

The clarity and pertinence of her comments were such a
delight that I immediately called to thank her. Finally, here
was someone who had a clue as to what our workload
entailed, and who offered useful, practical help. We bonded
instantly – two wholly dedicated people, hundreds of kilometres apart, yet on the same wavelength. She spoke with
such confidence and wisdom that I immediately saw her as a
mentor, picturing her as a kind, elderly woman with a bun of
white hair and an outdated wardrobe.

When I eventually met her, I did a double-take; I couldn't
believe this youthful blonde in jeans was the woman I'd been
talking to all this time. She acted just like a student, cracking
unprofessorial jokes and never hesitating to put her nose to
the grindstone, no matter how tedious the task. *She's one of
us*, I thought.

But what was best about working with her was how well
we complemented each other.

The daughter of a Holocaust survivor, Wendy knew that
silence was complicity, and she approached everything in an

outspoken, straightforward fashion. She seemed to think at twice the normal speed, and when confronted with criticism, she always bit back with the perfect answer, tight and unshakable. She also has a terrific sense of humour, which proved invaluable when things got bleak.

Unlike Wendy, I lacked a sense of vision that reached beyond the microcosm of the school. But I was a great learner, determined and very organized. Which came in handy for, as structured as her thinking was, Wendy's more practical skills were, shall we say, non-existent.

I realized it the first time I visited her at home in Toronto. From the verandah to the bathroom sink, no horizontal surface had been left uncluttered. The floor was strewn with books, newspapers, and toys, and the dining-room furniture could barely be seen under piles of paper and unlabelled diskettes. The darkness didn't help; many of her light bulbs were burned out.

The combination was ideal. For the first time since the tragedy, we both felt pulled up to a higher level.

᠊ᢦᢣᡃᢦ

By the end of March, the petition had just broken all Canadian records, and even pundits who doubted the political weight of signatures on crumpled sheets had to admit that half a million names was a lot of support.

But as impressive as this was, we knew that banning military weapons wouldn't be enough to ensure effective gun control. If we wanted a complete and comprehensive law, many other measures would have to be recommended.

With the help of crime-fighting authorities, Wendy had come up with a solid position, supporting such measures as registering all rifles and shotguns, licensing owners, increasing restrictions on handguns, and improving storage. When the teachers who had helped create the petition took it upon themselves to write our brief to the minister of justice, I naturally assumed that they would use her research.

Blame it on naïveté, but after my experience with the student congress, I should have known that it wouldn't go that smoothly.

⁂

"We have not attempted to describe and ban certain types of guns; instead, we proposed to specify the end to which their owners can put them. Indeed, current rapid technological changes teach us that this would be futile when applied to guns, just like it increasingly is in many other areas."

"They can't be serious!"

It was early evening and I was sitting on my bed, papers spread all around me. At the other end of the line, Wendy's voice hovered between irritation and amusement. She had just read the draft of the teachers' brief that I had faxed her, and if she hadn't known it was the work of university professors, she would have laughed her head off.

"Yes they are," I said. "Somehow, these two guys have decided that they're to be the sole authors of the brief. They're sorry they didn't retain your suggestions, but they did find you 'very charming.'"

"What am I, a flowerpot? Don't they know my proposals were put forward by experts in the field?"

I rolled my eyes. "They don't care. They said not to worry, they will take care of everything. I'd be surprised if they even read your notes."

"Typical. They sound like all the gun groups that favour unlimited licensing!"

"Yeah, as long as everyone is properly trained. Can you believe they don't even mention the ban on assault weapons?"

"*That's the core of the petition!* You're not going to let them get away with it, are you?"

"Me? What can *I* do?"

As a professor herself, Wendy wasn't put off by the arrogance of these teachers. I was. One of them was a teacher of mine, and I already wasn't doing well in his class – precisely because of all the time I spent on the petition. I couldn't tell him his work was trash two weeks before the finals!

She must have guessed what I was thinking.

"You can't let them get away with it," she said. "I'll give you a list of revisions, but you're the one who'll have to put a foot down."

"It's too late, they've already taken over! How about if I threaten to quit?"

"What good will that be? Listen to me. You represent the

student association on this issue. Your opinion carries much more weight than theirs. The issue is not whether you should bail out, it's whether you'll let the teachers stay *in*."

"You don't know what you're asking. They'll freak out!"

"Doesn't change a thing. You can't do any less than that."

My heart sank. But she was right, I couldn't back down.

Lying on my bed, I stared at the ceiling for a long, long time. This was where the path parted – the petition versus my studies, a far-away ideal versus an immediate benefit.

After a lot of soul-searching, I called one of the volunteers to assist me.

Mariette knew that my relationship with the professors was rocky, but she was astounded to learn that they intended to undermine the very spirit of the petition. Since her literary abilities were better than my own, she promptly came over to help me put my thoughts on paper.

It took us all night, but we managed to put everything down in a letter addressed to both teachers.

Dear Sirs,

On April 9, 1990, the minister of justice, the Honourable Kim Campbell, will come to l'École Polytechnique to meet the students. Deeply affected by the events of December 6, they will let her know how they feel about gun control in our country, and their reflections will be backed by an imposing number of signatures. . . .

Our committee will represent the 500,000 people that have endorsed the petition. But if its position does not match the signatories' intentions, then it cannot claim to be mandated by them, nor use the petition to endorse different objectives. . . .

This being said, I believe that, in its current state, the brief is both incomplete and unsatisfactory. In the first place, the emphasis should be put on what our support is about, namely, the ban on military and paramilitary weapons. It is with this type of gun that Lépine killed fourteen of our classmates. WE DON'T WANT THESE WEAPONS TO BE AVAILABLE ANY MORE, no matter what a "tighter" control system might be. . . .

Secondly, gun associations have had undue influence on the writing of the brief. Too much attention is spent on the "legitimate" possession of firearms. The case for better controls, in particular, is inadequately researched; except for certain nuances, it bears a curious resemblance to the arguments of the gun lobby.

Our demands are attached, along with a list of points which should be corrected or added. . . . It's not too late to modify the brief. Preserving months of work is much more significant than two or three evenings of overtime. . . .

My position is shared by all the students who worked with me. It would be deplorable if we had to question the credibility of the committee by publicly pointing out the lack of collaboration between its different members.

I hope that you will not neglect these comments.

I did not plan to send this off until I absolutely had to, but the act of writing, in and of itself, let me put my concerns into words that I could use as needed. I showed it to my team of student volunteers, making sure they all stood by me.

I also had it read by Louise Viau, a criminal law professor from the University of Montreal who had been our legal adviser since the petition's inception. If she and Alain both hadn't promised to stand by me as we went to discuss the brief with the professors, my determination would surely have suffered.

When I stepped into the teachers' lounge, the two professors were cheerful – they probably thought I'd ask for a new word here, a change of phrase there, and little more. But when, in a quavering voice, I told them I disagreed with most of their document, the colour swiftly disappeared from their faces.

I took a deep breath and mustered all of my resolve. I explained why we had to abide by the petitioners' wishes, and insisted on the need to incorporate the experts' advice into our position, all the while keeping my eyes down and fiddling with my papers as if it wasn't me talking. Being well-prepared didn't make it any easier – I couldn't believe I was lecturing my own professor!

Neither could he. Taut and stiff with anger, he stood up in the middle of my remarks, and yelled something like: "WHO DO YOU THINK YOU ARE!? You don't *know* what you're talking about, so *how dare you* question our abilities? In any case, there's *no time* left to make these kinds of changes!"

He turned to Alain and Louise, expecting them to back him. When they supported me instead, he didn't stay to argue. He grabbed his papers, stomped out of the room and slammed the door.

I was floored – I hadn't expected a tantrum from such an authority figure. For a few seconds, I didn't know what to say or do next.

Louise, however, had witnessed plenty of histrionics in her profession, and was unfazed by the outburst. Without missing a beat, she addressed the remaining professor.

"If you don't mind my saying so, sir, there is indeed little time left. Shall we get right down to business?"

Confounded, the man looked at the door. He hesitated for a few seconds, turned to me and took out his pen.

"Fine," he sighed. "What do you want changed?"

❧

The final version was far from perfect, but it covered the essentials. I took it as a rehearsal: this wouldn't be the last time I'd have to fight unexpected adversaries.

Wendy flew in early for the event. She met most of the volunteers, boxed the petitions with them, and gave a hand with the press kit. She didn't land a role in the proceedings – and the teachers pointedly ignored her – but the rest of us got along famously.

When we presented the petition to Kim Campbell, Alain did all the talking on behalf of the students, and I led the procession that handed over the boxes to the minister. She made a general promise for new gun-control legislation, and everyone was satisfied.

❧

My final exam in my teacher's class was a near bust: my mark was one point below the C average, sending me a dubious message about the consequences of defying his authority. But at least I passed!

The lousy mark didn't affect my career: I had already been guaranteed a job months earlier as a external-system designer at Bell Canada. The work wouldn't start until the fall, so I treated myself to a backpacking summer in Europe, and banished the last few months from my mind.

It felt good.

7

"Nothing could have prevented this tragedy from happening."

— Public Security Minister Sam Elkas

There was something liberating about travelling through seven countries in six weeks with nothing but a backpack, a train pass, and twenty-five dollars a day. I went from a state of perpetual worry (the petition, my studies, my extracurricular activities) to the simple concerns of trying to find an affordable bed for each night . . . and seeing as much as I could along the way.

I made all the mandatory stops, from Notre-Dame of Paris to the Prado of Madrid to the fortress of Beja to the Biergärten of Munich. But it's the little details I remember most: getting lost in narrow Portuguese alleyways that looked run down, yet led to flowery courtyards. Savouring a glass of sangria in an outdoor café on an enormous plaza while all the locals disappeared for the afternoon siesta. Watching an opera performed by Flemish marionettes clad in more refined clothes than I would wear in my entire life. Visiting the independent "republic" of Christiania in downtown Copenhagen, where hippies sell their pot unencumbered.

It goes without saying that my journey was all the better when shared with fellow travellers – for the companionship, the travel tips, and the shared accommodations. When I got to Mount Jungfrau, for example, I was able to stay at the booked-up youth hostel only because all the latecomers were allowed to take over the main lounge for the night.

I soon found that, regardless of the time and distance, the shootings were never far from people's minds. One day, I was waiting in line to sign up for a couple of tours when this American jock tried to strike up a conversation by inquiring where I came from and what I did. All I had to do was answer "Montreal, civil engineering" and his eyes nearly popped out.

"You heard about the massacre?"

"Yes. I was there."

"Holy fuck! You're kidding!"

His macho stance turned to awkward concern on the spot.

"*Man!* I can't tell you how that got to me. I was in a pub with my friends when they talked about it on the TV over the bar. Nobody believed it at first, until they showed us the images. Fourteen girls! Terrible shit."

It was the same scene with two other backpackers, a little before the lights were switched off. Deaken was one of those Australians who make the most of what may be their only trip abroad, and he had been hopping from one hostel to the next for over a year. He was in Florence when he heard a bunch of fellow travellers reading aloud from *USA Today* (the only American paper that's available everywhere in

Europe – and, by sheer coincidence, one of the rare publications that had quoted me). Since most of the backpackers
were themselves students or recent graduates, they were all
horrified by the news.

Keiko was a tiny Japanese girl, rather shy, whose parents
were rich enough to pay for as many trips as she wanted.
They had told her what happened at the supper table, and
since gun-related violence is extremely rare in her country,
she had had a hard time believing that firearms could be so
easily available, especially in a country with as peaceful a reputation as Canada.

It kept happening through my entire trip: I'd mention
where I came from, and people would tell me precisely
where they were when they first got the news. Even today,
the people I meet never fail to relate how they heard about
the massacre.

Compared to the thousands of people who die every day
from accidents or diseases, the fourteen victims received a
disproportionate amount of attention. It may have been due
to the strength of what it symbolized, that sexual equality was
much frailer than we all had presumed. It may have been
because this kind of horror isn't supposed to happen to
people so young, or in the peaceful confines of a learning
institution. Or was it simply because such unexpected and
sudden violence made everyone feel more vulnerable and
every parent more fearful?

In any case, the fight for tougher controls was no longer a
student crusade to me. The massacre had brought Poly to the
frontlines, but I now saw that the whole country was living a

lie. How could we expound on peaceful values while we were selling machine guns to teenagers?

᠅

I didn't know how big a change our petition would bring about, but for a few weeks after my return, my preoccupations were more immediate.

I found a small apartment, worked out a budget to pay off my student debts, and underwent a long-overdue operation on my knee (which had taken the brunt of a dozen sports accidents). The trauma of open surgery caused unexpected hardening of the tissues, and I was unable to bend my leg for much longer than the normal six months' healing period. When I started work, I did so on crutches.

It was a harrowing experience. My limb was permanently stuck at an awkward 110 degrees, and between my physiotherapy sessions I had to limit its movement in order not to aggravate my condition. Yet I needed to go out every other day in order to measure long distances along roads and construction sites, and the pain grew worse with every limp. Back at the office, the mere idea of getting up to consult a report made me shudder so much that I would put it off until it became squarely unavoidable.

The other half of the job was rather easy, though. I was enlisted in a special program for high-management prospects, had a full-time clerk working for me and spent many days attending technical courses and leadership workshops. I knew I was lucky to have landed this position. And I would have applied myself with genuine dedication if it hadn't been for the more important issues on my mind. The legislation that we were promised had been tabled, and it did nothing to lift my spirits.

I'd never seen a bill before, but given my interest, I thought I'd get through it without too much trouble. But, like most people who aren't familiar with legal texts, I found the language nearly impossible to decipher.

A sample of Bill C-80:

101. (1) Whenever a peace officer believes on reasonable grounds that an offence is being committed or has been committed against any of the provisions of this Act relating to prohibited weapons, restricted weapons, firearms or ammunition and that evidence of the offence is likely to be found on a person, in a vehicle or in any place or premises other than a dwelling-house, the peace officer may, where the conditions for obtaining a warrant exist but, by reason of exigent circumstances, it would not be practical to obtain a warrant, search, without warrant, the person, vehicle, place or premises, and may seize anything by means of or in relation to which that officer believes on reasonable grounds the offence is being committed or has been committed.

(Yes, that *is* a single sentence.)

Despite my passion for the cause, my eyes kept glazing over – this gobbledegook went on for pages and pages! But I got the hang of what the bill was saying. Now my distaste stemmed from the content, not the syntax.

The bill could be reduced to four minor changes to the current gun law: it raised the cost of the Firearm Acquisition Certificate; it asked applicants to list two references; it created a twenty-eight-day cooling-off period before the FAC was granted; and it limited the number of bullets a magazine can hold. It did *not* include a ban on assault weapons. Many, like the semi-automatic versions of the Uzi and the AK-47, were simply reclassified as "restricted," like handguns, but the Ruger Mini-14 was not even on *that* list.

Such pathetic proposals should have made me angry. Politicians had expressed how shocked they were that a massacre of this magnitude had happened in Canada. They had assured us that they would do everything in their power to prevent a similar tragedy. And all they could produce were these paltry measures?

I *should* have been angry, but I wasn't. Now that the petition was over, I felt helpless once again, and the bill simply confirmed that one couldn't beat the system. How could I ever have presumed that we'd get more than these crumbs?

Yet Wendy still did. She had expanded her network of experts, collected information about the controls in other countries, published a critique of the bill, and called for letters demanding its strengthening – an impressive start for a single mom with little time on her hands.

She had started by calling a police inspector who had been quoted in the papers, and she had explained about her objectives. He referred her to his higher-up, who, while she was still sitting in his office, called another chief.

"There's this woman here who's working on gun control," he said, as if surprised that a citizen showed an interest. "You really should hear this, she's got it down pat. Shall I send her over?"

A few days later, she had received her first letter of support. Then, a criminologist invited her to speak at their annual convention, which in turn connected her to a church council on justice issues, and the networking continued from then on.

It was time *I* got back on the horse.

There were plenty of opportunities: I kept getting calls from public-affairs programs, members of Parliament, and perfect strangers who wanted to encourage me. But even though I firmly believed in my position, I could scarcely see why I warranted so much attention. I had no formal expertise and I was *not* a born orator.

Until I understood that people counted on me to defend the views of ordinary Canadians – no more, no less. My intervention were not only welcome, but essential to counter what the gun enthusiasts were saying. All I had to do was imagine the listeners who wanted to see them put in their place, and my convictions would win over my doubts.

The debate promised to be highly colourful . . . but not always very clean. When I faced the president of the Quebec Wildlife Federation on television, he brazenly claimed that all firearms were already registered, so what were we whining about? Of course this was completely false, and when I pointed it out to him, he shrugged me off. He didn't give a damn about any gun victims, he told me when the show was over. All he cared about was blocking our stupid controls.

I had to hide behind some equipment for a few moments in order to regain my composure. Were we really up against such callous people?

If that's the way the game was played, I realized I had to be ready for anything.

It felt like cramming for another exam: I read all I could find on the subject, and used every spare moment to improve my arguments – I even brought my notes into the washroom at work. I wore out several highlighters, boiled the material down to short summaries and prepared bite-sized answers to the most common objections.

Myths and Facts about Gun Control

"Guns don't kill people, people kill people."
• Guns are 15 times more lethal than knives, and much deadlier than fists.
• When a gun is involved, a domestic dispute is 12 times more likely to end in death.
• Suicides are 5 times more likely to occur in homes with guns – these being the means that are most likely (92%) to lead to death.
"People need guns for protection."
• Self-protection, as a rule, is not a legal reason for buying a gun in Canada.
• A gun in the home is 43 times more likely to kill a family member than an intruder.

- Out of the 24,000 total handgun deaths in the U.S. in one year, only 178 occurred in cases of self-defence.

"Cars kill more people than guns."

- People use cars on a daily basis; guns are more lethal on a per-use basis.
- If the law was as strict with guns as it is with cars, we'd already have tough controls.

"We should fight crime, not gun owners."

- Most homicide victims are killed by family members or acquaintances, often without premeditation.
- Guns most often recovered from crimes are common rifles and shotguns – very few are smuggled over the border.
- Registration will allow the police to distinguish illegal from legally-owned firearms, and charge illegal owners accordingly.

"A registered gun kills just as easily."

- If police could trace guns back to their last legal owners, illegal transfers would be harder to get away with, thereby shrinking the black market and preventing crime. Registration would help the police carry out the 17,000 court orders which, every year, oblige them to seize all the guns in someone's possession.

"Controls don't work in other countries."

- In the year that followed the December 6 massacre, handguns were used to murder 10 people in Australia, 13 in Sweden, and 22 in Great Britain.
- In the U.S., where they were more freely available, 10,567 people were murdered by handguns.

It called for a lot of work, but it was worth it. I knew I'd be facing older men in suits and ties, and I had to make sure that my opinions would carry more weight than theirs.

Like most people who don't work in the field, I never got to like my on-air interventions. (Even today, I try to avoid them.)

It also took me a while to stop letting myself be intimidated by journalists. Faced with such powerful players, I only later decided that I didn't *have* to answer all of their questions. Privacy and restraint are one's to own and protect, never mind the public's "right to know." On every anniversary of the tragedy, reporters would expect me to express my feelings about it – preferably with tears. I never would.

And I accepted that it was absolutely fine to be ignorant about certain things. Surviving an attack did not make me an expert on every related subject, like the compensation of crime victims, or the parole system. And I certainly didn't want to be quoted on a different issue than the one I cared about.

But all this did make me follow current events with more interest, even when guns weren't involved. I noticed the different ways in which the various media covered the same story, and I became aware of occasional mistakes, omissions, or biases – which often reflected the personalities of the journalists, or the editorial position of their superiors.

Everything got closer and more concrete for me. The papers and news programs no longer seemed like monoliths that kept the public at arm's length; I discovered they were the sum total of hundreds of contacts between regular people, on both sides of the microphones.

Unfortunately, the important things aren't always reported by the media. Our opponents, for instance, had used their strongest tactic as soon as the bill was tabled: they took their complaints to individual members of Parliament.

In theory, we should still have had a numerical advantage on that front. But when it came to well-orchestrated protest campaigns, our opponents were well ahead of us. They already had a wide network of stores, clubs, and associations to support their goals; we were barely getting started. They hired professional lobbyists; we depended on untrained volunteers. They felt their personal interests were threatened; we defended a general concept with no immediate benefits.

In the blink of an eye, gun owners everywhere had been prodded into action, and their MPs had been flooded with letters, phone calls, and visits. Under constant attack, they began fearing political reprisals if they supported Campbell's bill, and they quickly reconsidered backing her proposals.

Then came the bombshell. On November 24, 1990, Kim Campbell announced that she was sending Bill C-80 to a "Special Committee" for re-evaluation. I didn't understand what that meant at first. But I found out soon enough.

A bill normally goes through three official phases. First reading takes place when it's tabled in the House. Second reading is when parliamentarians discuss its main features, vote on principle, and send the draft to a committee of MPs for outside input. Third reading occurs when a fine-tuned version returns to the House for a final vote. If the Senate approves it through a similar process, it receives final assent and becomes law.

The entire process must take place before the end of the parliamentary session, for that's when the agenda is cleared. Beyond that, everything must be re-submitted from step one.

What had just occurred with Bill C-80, I learned, was most extraordinary. Since the gun lobby had managed to deprive Campbell of the necessary support within her own party, she had invoked a need for further studies and taken the bill off the usual agenda *before* it even got to second reading.

The pretext was transparent: the Special Committee would never be able to report back before the end of the current session. The gun lobby had won; the bill was as good as dead.

YEAR TWO

8

Q: Why does anyone need an AK-47?
A: Why does anyone need a Corvette?

– Member of the Special Committee to
Don Hinchley, president of Safeguard

Some said that the minister's timing was intentional, that it was a disguised cry for help.

When she made it known that she was referring the bill to a special committee, she must have foreseen that it would scandalize everyone affected by the killings. Withdrawing the bill twelve days before the first anniversary of the tragedy may have been an attempt to get the public to renew its pressure for gun control.

It certainly was a wake-up call for Wendy and me. We hadn't even seen the other runners race to the finish line, and we were now eating their dust.

Stunned and despondent, we got together to take stock of the situation. I must confess, I was tempted to consider the struggle hopeless and retreat into blissful inertia. But I would have had to ignore all the calls from people who insisted that something had to be done.

But what exactly could be done . . . and who would be doing it? Since Wendy had already designed a form letter in support of a stronger bill, she suggested we build a postal offensive around it.

"Are you still the students' spokesperson? We could get the victims' parents to write letters, and get everyone to follow suit. . . ."

I wasn't so sure. Back at the school, the members of the student council had finished their term at the end of May, taking with them their passion for the cause. The new council didn't see gun control as part of their mandate and now that I had graduated, I could hardly act on their behalf.

So I borrowed a large table from my sister next door, and I invited to my small apartment the half-dozen people I knew who were most interested in gun control, including two of one victim's relatives, Suzanne Laplante-Edward and her son Jimmy.

A strong-willed woman, dressed in colours as bold as her words were candid, Suzanne was the first parent to come out of her state of mourning with a sense of mission. Spirited, flamboyant, determined, and passionate, she had no patience for the opponents of gun control, and could light a fire under any crowd that she addressed (which she would do innumerable times in the years to come). It was a way of keeping the memory of her daughter alive, a battle in which she was prepared to invest all of her energy.

Though our goal was clear – to press the government into recommitting to gun control – our combined political *savoir faire* was rather embryonic. We ended up rallying around Wendy's suggestion and, by the time the pizzas arrived, we had worked out the basic tenets of a letter-writing campaign aimed at the prime minister.

Spurred on by Suzanne's enthusiasm for the project, I spent the rest of the week collecting the other victims' relatives' signatures (a total of 129) on a joint letter to Brian Mulroney. The student leaders agreed to distribute the form letter back at their schools, Montreal *Gazette* writer Jack Todd filed no less than three columns in support of our campaign, and Wendy and I set out to place the letter in as many newspapers as possible. If the editor felt like it, we suggested, the text could be presented like a coupon, to be clipped, signed and sent in.

It was an outlandish idea – newspapers don't ordinarily publish that kind of thing unless it's a paid advertisement. So whenever we had a chance, we got on the phone, asked to speak to the editor, and pleaded for free space. When we couldn't get free space, we begged supporters to donate the cost of an ad.

One of the people I called was my dean, who immediately pledged a big contribution. I didn't know that he was just about to give a press conference to unveil the school's annual report. But when the journalists there showed more interest in what he had to say about what had happened to the gun-control bill, he turned to François Legendre, the new student president, and praised him to high heaven for the efforts that *we* were making.

The cameras clicked away as François put on his best face and went along with the story. Within twelve hours, his picture had found its way on the front page of the *Gazette*: STUDENTS WILL PRESS ON FOR GUN LAW, the headline clamoured.

Seeing our efforts announced like that laid to rest the residual doubts I still harboured. *We're front-page news*, I thought. *This campaign might actually work!* My mandate as spokesperson for the students was hurriedly renewed by the student council, and I fell to the task without delay.

In anticipation of the upcoming anniversary, every journalist looking for a new angle latched onto this development. Since Wendy and I led the only groups that demanded gun control, interviews were lined up days in advance, and we used all these occasions to call for support.

To our delight, the mail-in campaign was a huge success. We announced the publication of the form letter in at least a dozen newspapers during a press conference in Poly's entrance hall, and mountains of mail would later be delivered to the prime minister.

I was so excited, I kept telling my co-workers at Bell, "Guess what? An MP wants to meet with me! Look! They're talking about us in the papers!" But all I got in return were puzzled stares, as if they were looking for a connection with company business. My colleagues were unimpressed with what was going on. The company encouraged social activities, but they meant those which benefited the business, such as office outings and employee fundraisers. They weren't paying me to lobby for gun control, were they?

I toned down my enthusiasm. Earning little response at the office while I made waves on a national scale was a bit of a cold shower, but so what? The adrenalin rush was back, and I felt more useful than I had in a long time.

❧

When the justice minister's Special Committee began its review of the dying bill, the student association was invited to present its point of view.

I knew so little about what was entailed by such a request that I had put it on the back burner until the letter-writing campaign was over and done with. If anything, I thought I'd be one of many people lining up to deliver a brief statement. After the cavalcade of reporters I'd just survived, it didn't seem like a very big deal.

Was I ever wrong! Two days before I was to appear before the committee, I asked around about what I should expect, and learned that the affair would be much more formal than I'd thought. I'd have to submit a position paper, which would be closely scrutinized. The students' views and recommendations would be weighed against those of the pro-gun groups, and the committee would ask pointed questions about any imprecision or contradiction it perceived. All of our statements would be entered on the record, and copies would remain accessible to anyone for years to come.

I suddenly felt overwhelmed – but Louise reassured me by recommending that I keep it short anyway. Committee

members had to deal with a lot of inflated prose, and they
would appreciate a concise presentation. In other words, I
should simply elaborate on the five or six themes that made
up the core of our form letter:

Bill C-80 does offer improvements over existing controls.
However, it clearly leans in favour of the gun lobby. We feel
that an acceptable compromise should include the following points:

Treat gun ownership as a privilege, not a right. The
bill prohibits gun ownership only for people convicted of
an indictable offence involving violence and carrying a
maximum sentence of 10 years or more. This does not
include most violent assaults, wife-beating or the most
serious drug offences, like trafficking. *These offences should
be included in the bill.*

The bill also includes exemptions. But we have yet to
imagine a circumstance in which a person who perpe-
trated a crime with intent to kill should be allowed to own
a gun. *These exemptions should be removed from the bill.*

A privilege must be earned. The bill does entitle firearms officers to refuse a request considering the violent
or criminal background of an applicant, but the officer
has to prove that this person must not own a gun. *The
applicant should be the one to prove that he needs the gun
and that he is safe.*

**Fix eighteen as the minimum age for the purchase of a
gun.** A teenager who cannot drink or vote should not be
allowed to purchase a gun. Period.

Remove existing paramilitary weapons from circulation. The bill only bans certain combat weapons, and "grandfather clauses" allow people to keep those in circulation. Yet none of the owners that we talked to was able to give us a reason for allowing these weapons, except for "the awesome feeling they give when you hold them." Of course, there are collectors, but how are they different from any person who wants to have more guns? The bill does not define what a collector is.

Record gun types and serial numbers. A national registry is essential. It would match existing registry on cars and their owners and make purchasers more responsible for their firearms, their storage and their use. Most guns used for criminal intent have at one time been legally owned.

Require the permit to purchase ammunition. A simple and effective step, it would at least keep ammunition out of the hands of those who possess illegal firearms.

Improve controls on storage. The bill only requires collectors of restricted weapons to provide evidence of safe storage. Why not all guns? In addition, it should define what safe storage is, and provide a mechanism by which police can check the result.

We view these requests as the bare minimum for an effective gun-control law. Such a law would not prevent legitimate hunters and target shooters from owning weapons. But it would require gun owners to be responsible, and it would ban the weapons which have no purpose other than to wound and kill human beings with murderous efficiency.

The result wasn't an in-depth analysis, but given the time
constraints, it was a decent piece of work. Wendy would
supplement it on behalf of Canadians for Gun Control
with a thicker brief a few days later, and the victims'
parents would make a powerful presentation of their own
(though they had to kick up a storm to be heard, for the
committee "felt it would be too hurtful" for the relatives to
relive the event).

As for presenting our testimony, I wouldn't be alone. To
make the delegation more official, two other students came
along: François Legendre, the president of the Polytechnique
student association, and Dawn Wiseman, representing the
Congress of Canadian Engineering Students. They would
describe our history and support, while I would state our
demands and answer questions.

Unfortunately, I wasn't in the best physical condition
when I arrived at the Parliament buildings – I was still relying
on crutches to get around, and a night of hectic discussion in
the hotel prior to our morning presentation hadn't let me
catch more than a few winks, so my body was demanding I
make up for lost sleep.

My unease worsened when we entered the committee
room. It was *much* bigger than I had expected, a high-
ceilinged hall decked out with sombre portraits and crests.
Translators sat in a corner booth. There were rows of desks
for reporters, seats with earphones for the audience, and a
rectangular arrangement of tables for the MPs, with five
chairs for the witnesses. Very unnerving. I felt like we were
being put under a microscope.

Did I just say five chairs? Surprise! Our presentation had been lumped with that of the two teachers, who were re-submitting the same old brief!

For a moment, I just gaped at the set-up. Over in the audience, Wendy was already writing a note, which she passed to an incoming committee member. This was no time for a replay of last spring's skirmish, but she wanted the committee warned that professors and students were different groups with distinct petitions.

Good thing, too, because the teachers' presentation did not win them any friends. They took the microphone away from us several times and fumbled badly when pressed for statistics that backed their claims. When one MP asked us how we would respond to a certain pro-gun argument, they lashed out at him, as if *he* were siding with our opponents!

"First of all," they snapped, "we've met with your people, your organization –"

"It is *not* my organization."

"You said your people, members of clubs . . ."

"I said 'members of my community'!"

Everyone was taken aback by the outburst, for the meeting should have been an exercise in diplomacy. We were here to demonstrate the validity of our position, not to attack politicians who were seeking our opinions!

The MP who was given Wendy's message read it and passed it on to his colleagues. From then on they specified whose answers they were seeking – the students' or the teachers'. It enabled me to reply on behalf of the students without fear of interruption, and I relaxed.

If not for the teachers, the whole exercise wouldn't have been anywhere near the ordeal I was told it would be. Instead of an elaborate grilling or trick questions, I got reasonably straightforward inquiries along the lines of:

"You want all firearms to be stored safely. But how could such a regulation be enforced? We can't send someone to every household. . . ." I told them it should be on par with enforcing the drunk-driving law. While the police can do verifications in some circumstances, the law itself will be enough of an incentive for most people.

"Do you insist on having all semi-automatics considered restricted weapons, or simply the high-powered ones?"

I replied that once a task force has determined what legitimate uses there were, the corresponding guns could remain available, with severe restrictions on their ownership. All others should be banned.

"An argument is made over and over that if we strengthen the penalties, people will not use these guns in a criminal way. What is your reaction?" I said when one kills out of rage, a severe sanction means little. The important thing is to keep guns out of the hands of potentially dangerous people.

I kept thinking "nothing to it" and "you must know already know the answer to this one" until I finally caught on. Sympathetic MPs were just helping me get our points on the record, and the others didn't want to appear mean to the students. Talk about an ego boost! When the chair said "Ladies and gentlemen, we would like to thank you," I was almost disappointed.

I tried to stay and chat with the committee members and their staff, but some people kept steering me towards the exit. I wondered whether it was considered bad manners to hang around in the room for too long, until I gave up, opened the doors – and the world exploded into light.

"What will happen to the bill?"

"How did the MPs respond?"

"What do you plan to do next?"

There must have been five camera crews and three times as many journalists out there, all of them rushing at me and shouting and thrusting spotlights in my face. I couldn't see or hear anything except white streaks and jumbled roars, and I just stood there, stunned, for what must have been ten long seconds. I hadn't been warned, I was completely unprepared, I didn't know what to say!

Wake up, Heidi, this is all going to be on the air tonight.

"Uh..."

Choose a question. Focus on one reporter.

Then I found my voice:

"Well, the committee members listened carefully to our concerns. We hope they will support our recommendations, which are..."

Much better. Plant your message. Do your job.

That's when it sank in ... this *was* my job.

9

"You don't hide firearms from children. You gun-proof your child. It's easy to educate a child to a point where they are quite safe with firearms."

– Dave Tomlinson, president, National Firearms Association

One of the perks of the hearings was that it gave us the opportunity finally to meet our opponents in the flesh.

Until now, the term "gun lobby" had failed to give me a precise image of the other side, other than a shady conglomerate that blocked everything that threatened its interests. We knew about their members, their arguments, and their publications, but we had never been able to put faces on the decision-makers at the helm of the group.

The encounter was mercifully brief. I had no sooner returned to the committee room after being quizzed by the media than a tall, bearded fellow and a small, white-haired man cornered Wendy and I at the door. We had noticed them earlier when we tried to identify everyone in the room, but we hadn't been able to place them with any degree of certainty. Reporters usually have media passes hanging around their necks and sit closer to the committee, while civil servants and aides are . . . well, more sharply dressed. Jeans and frumpy suits don't quite cut it with this crowd.

We did recognize the men's names as soon as they introduced themselves, however. It would have been hard not to: they were behind most of the rhetoric that we had read against gun control.

"Heidi and Wendy? Dave Tomlinson."

"Mike Martinoff."

So these were the mighty warriors of the National Firearms Association who posed as the leaders of the Canadian gun community. Since they had defeated the bill so easily, I'd have expected them to pass us by without a glance. Yet here they stood, chatting us up as if we were old business partners.

It might have been an interesting experience if we had perceived the slightest charm, manner, or wit. But I found no pleasure in being thrown string after string of obscure statistics and arguable data, right from the start.

Oh, they shared our concerns, they truly did. But the world they were describing was very different from our own – a world where criminals reigned supreme and where the police was incapable of ensuring our protection. According to them, a tougher law would only benefit the black market and render people more vulnerable to the attacks of violent offenders.

I saw them coming a mile away: *An armed society is a polite society. We don't protect victims by making them unable to protect themselves.* I braced myself for the usual lecture about fighting criminals, not guns. I had been down this road so many times, there wasn't much they could say that would be news to either of us, let alone make us change our minds.

"Uh, yes, I'm familiar with that theory, but I believe –"

I never got any further: they were already offering to take us to lunch and "explain" everything. They said they understood that our intentions were good, but they also knew how confusing the subject could be to those of us who didn't know guns.

"Thanks, but sorry. I don't think that would make any diff –"

They, on the other hand, dealt with guns all the time, and if we gave them a chance, they were sure we'd be impressed with all their amassed expertise.

Throughout this one-sided conversation, I kept backing up to maintain my personal space, and I was halfway across the room when I caught sight of an acquaintance and pointed him out to Wendy. We bid the two men goodbye and got out of there before they could prod us any further.

I really should thank them, though. In just a few minutes, they did more to bolster my self-assurance than all the praise that had been heaped on us since the beginning. They had more confidence in our capabilities than I had.

If they saw us as a genuine threat, then our work must be worth reckoning with.

⁂

After a few more weeks of conflict between my responsibilities at work and my commitment to the cause, I finally reached my breaking point.

The game of hide-and-seek that I played with my employer had become unbearable. I'd talk on the phone in low tones to camouflage my calls, I'd return gun control–related messages first and business ones second, and I was always asking for personal photocopying and long-distance privileges – which, to his credit, my boss grudgingly granted (the company even donated a fax machine). But I could see that everyone at the office was annoyed, and since I normally take pride in what I do, so was I.

Before I even landed my first summer job (shovelling manure in a local stable), my father had instilled rigorous values in me and my sisters. Refrain from cutting corners. Don't postpone what you can do right away. Never leave a job unfinished.

To my dismay, I was now breaking all of these commandments, and the worst thing was, I was doing it both as an office worker *and* as an activist. I couldn't even tell which weighed more heavily on my conscience any more: was it that I had failed to bring about what our petition had outlined, or that I had become a poor employee?

Something had to give. One of my co-workers took me aside one day, and tried to beat some sense into me. A graduate from Polytechnique herself, she was in the same training program I was in, and very intent on staying on board.

"Heidi, you have to make up your mind. If you want to succeed in this company, you have to give it your all, and that could mean sacrificing things you care about. Look at me: I've made my choice. I gave up some hobbies and lost sight of a few friends, but I have a great salary and a dream house with a big pool. You have to keep your eyes on the prize and sort your priorities accordingly."

Fair enough.

To do a good job on gun control, I needed to work on it full-time, earn enough to support myself, in a well-equipped office, in partnership with Wendy.

These conditions weren't the only problem. Aside from my work on the petition, I had no real experience in politics. Not to mention that, unlike cancer research or famine relief, gun control was seen by the private sector as too contentious an issue for them to support us financially. Our political activism made us ineligible for charitable status – donations to the cause would never qualify as tax deductions.

Put it all together, and finding enough sponsors wouldn't be an easy task.

It didn't really matter. I only had to contact one person.

꒰ꙮ꒱

Jocelyne

I've been exposed to death from a very early age.

Alfred Dallaire is a family-run enterprise that's been in the funeral business for three generations. Most people think this can render anybody impervious to human suffering; some cynics have even hinted that I got involved because the massacre was "good for business." To me, this is as ludicrous as saying that doctors welcome epidemics. Everyone dies one day or another. We don't need any help in that regard.

I'm in this line of work because I've been sensitized to distress. But when I heard about the killings, I reacted as a woman first. Horror, of course, as well as marked frustration. Fourteen dead, I thought. Maybe violence against women will now get a little airplay.

At the time, I was attending a benefit presided over by an alumni of Polytechnique. I went straight up to her and said I'd do anything her alma mater deemed fit. Two days later, I was invited over by the administrators and, since this was my field of expertise, my offer to handle the funeral arrangements was passed on to all of victims' families.

We eventually footed the entire bill – the government sent me a cheque to cover the costs, but I couldn't bring myself to cash it. What I did instead was create a foundation that would hand out annual bursaries to women engineers. Other donors joined in and, along with her friend Nathalie Provost, Heidi was selected as the very first beneficiary upon her graduation.

When she got back in touch six months later, I wasn't surprised at all to hear of her new battle plans. Her lack of political experience never even entered my mind: I knew she'd be the right person for the job.

❧

It felt so strange.

For years, I had wanted to become an engineer. I had studied like mad to earn my degree. I wanted to solve complex problems, manage huge construction projects and make a name for myself in the field. And now I was throwing it all away for a six-month offer – in a completely different sector.

I had no questions, no hesitations: I resigned the moment Jocelyne Légaré's offer came through. *I'm only giving up a job, not my entire career*, I kept telling myself. *This is just until a bill is passed.*

Which isn't to say that there was no sense of loss. Understandably, the phone company wouldn't be taking me back when I was done, and I wasn't looking forward to a new job hunt. The civil-engineering market wasn't exactly booming: many of my fellow graduates were still looking for work, and I didn't know how well I'd compete after my hiatus as an activist.

Announcing the whole thing to my parents was no picnic, either. After all, they had paid for most of my education, and they were quite alarmed when I told them I was withdrawing from engineering just as the dividends were beginning to roll in. Explaining about gun control was a moot point – like all good parents, their primary concern was my personal security, financial and otherwise. Their apprehensions shook me to the core, but I had to set them aside, hoping it would all work out in the long run.

I especially regretted leaving the mathematical universe behind – the way complex concepts interconnect, until a whole maze of abstract notions makes perfect sense, fascinates me. Given the kinds of arguments that were brought forth during the debates I attended, I knew I'd be forfeiting crisp irrefutable logic as soon as I took possession of my cubicle in Jocelyne's secretarial pool.

On the plus side, that was the day Wendy and I formally

merged our efforts. We retained separate offices in Toronto and Montreal, but we knew it was time to act as a single group. The Coalition for Gun Control was open for business.

As for Jocelyne, all she asked us was that her contribution be known. She had to have something to justify the initiative to the rest of her family. I certainly didn't mind. As long as it didn't affect our autonomy, she could shout about her generosity on every street corner in the city.

To ensure a successful public announcement of our new arrangement, she retained a high-priced PR firm.

Several meetings were held.

Time passed.

But nothing took shape.

Jocelyne's announcement was ultimately pared down to a single press release. And even that wouldn't have been picked up by the media if I hadn't personally called a local journalist's attention to it.

Though publicity hadn't been her primary goal, Jocelyne was understandably deflated. She proposed that her PR agency handle the Coalition's next press conference, in order to give them a second chance. At first I agreed, but then she came back and said they would need more time.

"No way," I said. "The government's agenda for the coming year will be made public in the Throne Speech next week, and since it probably won't include anything about gun control, we have to give an immediate response. If you don't mind, we'll take over from here."

She made a sceptical face, but Wendy and I immediately sprang into action.

We reserved a space on the top floor of the Radisson Hotel, overlooking Parliament Hill. We enlisted people to speak on behalf of national organizations most concerned with safety. We wrote a tentative script and faxed an invitation to all the news outlets we knew of.

We got a full house! Not only was it the first time groups had come together to make a plea for tougher controls, but our choice of location added to the originality of the event – experienced lobbyists generally use one of the Parliament's press rooms. There had been a definite leadership void on the issue, and everyone on the Hill – from reporters to MPs to bureaucrats – wanted to see who would fill it.

Wendy opened by denouncing the Throne Speech's silence on gun control. The president of the student association and I evoked Campbell's promises along with the support of the most important women's groups for a new law. Two doctors underscored the unanimity of the medical literature with respect to gun control's power to save lives. The spokesperson for the Canadian Association of Chiefs of Police said it was time to get our priorities in order and ban all assault weapons, while the Canadian Police Association brought up its concerns about the influence of the gun lobby. The Canadian Bar Association argued that the Charter provides a constitutional basis for our demands. The representative of the Canadian Criminal Justice Association emphasized the link between easy access to guns and their criminal misuse. And Jocelyne wrapped things up by calling on other companies to support us as hers did.

It wasn't the exclusive tribute that her company had hoped for, but since she was quoted in every article about the press conference, she certainly didn't object.

❧

The important thing was, the government had been persuaded. Even though it hadn't listed gun control among its priorities for the new session, a new bill was introduced in the House that very spring.

This time, Kim Campbell didn't wait for the objections to pile up. She now had enough support among her colleagues to push the bill through first and second readings, and she sent it posthaste to committee for further deliberation.

And she didn't stop there, either. We heard through the grapevine that she also planned to tell the committee members that enough consultation had been held by last winter's Special Committee. Further hearings, she'd instruct them, would be totally superfluous.

It sounded reasonable, but it was a sleight of hand. Her first bill had never reached second reading, and so the Special Committee, as well as the witnesses appearing before it, had only discussed whether it was *necessary* to legislate and had concluded that the proposals had merit. The new bill, however, was now past second reading and due for a detailed examination by a legislative committee.

The question was, were we so anxious to have a law – no matter how modest – that we would agree with the minister and bypass this crucial stage?

We weren't. Under its brand new wrapping, Bill C-17 was no different from the dead Bill C-80. A complete ban on assault weapons and the registration of rifles and shotguns were nowhere to be found.

Since it had already been approved in principle, we knew it was too late for substantial modifications, but if it skipped the committee stage altogether, we could kiss any small improvements goodbye as well.

After all our efforts to get a new bill tabled, we had to keep it from being rushed through.

10

"I need a large-capacity magazine to shoot the rabbits in my apple orchard."

– Arnold Malone, member of Parliament

"I never thought I'd say this, but just this once, we want the same thing as the gun guys."

Wendy shook her head.

"Our motives aren't exactly the same, are they?" she said. "We want hearings to improve the bill. They want a chance to destroy it altogether."

"I'm aware of that. But if we manage to derail the minister's plan, we may actually be helping the other side."

"So? Take a good hard look at the bill, and tell me that we should accept it as it is."

"Not a chance."

At this point, there had been no formal announcement of the minister's intention to skip the committee stage. All we were going on were rumours within the Justice Department. We couldn't denounce Campbell's intentions until she made them plain to the committee members. Yet we also had to intervene *before* they gave her an answer, for they might just agree with her and wrap up on the spot.

That left us a very small window of opportunity – during the first meeting of the Legislative Committee itself.

To prove that consultations were essential, we would have to identify problems with the bill and show that they could be addressed without altering the overall thrust. We'd need sample amendments, as well as evidence that these changes were very much in demand.

All this within one weekend – the minister's testimony was scheduled for Monday, June 17, 11 A.M.

Piece of cake.

※

The dissection of a bill is anything but fun, and a race against time only makes things worse.

We didn't complain – it would only have wasted valuable seconds. We entered a parallel state, where every move had to be carried out at top speed, and where the task at hand monopolized all of our thoughts. High on adrenalin, we virtually stopped eating and sleeping. And when exhaustion set in, our minds just switched to autopilot.

This was the state we were in throughout the weekend. Our one advantage was that we didn't have to burden ourselves with bureaucratic procedures or a rigid hierarchy. I made a few calls to fellow students, and soon had recruited a crack team of amateur legislators.

Christian, Sébastien, Nicolas and I highlighted the bill's gaps and loopholes.

Louise helped me formulate the amendments.

Wendy provided supporting arguments by fax.

François gave us the student association's stamp of approval.

And some poor guy who wanted to write a book about us was saddled with the proofreading and the translation.

We sweated and swore and gave up on sleep altogether, but as Monday dawned, our printer was spitting out the final pages:

POSSIBLE AMENDMENTS [*Excerpts*]

Purpose:

Eliminate all grandfathering clauses pertaining to exemptions from the ban on all converted automatic or fully automatic weapons.

Assault weapons serve no legitimate purpose. Police, legal and municipal associations have asked that these weapons be subjected to a ban without exemption.

Means:

– Eliminate converted automatic weapons from the definition of restricted weapons.

– Include all automatic weapons, converted or not converted, in the prohibited category.

– Correlatively abolish the subsection which requires a report to the Commissioner when such a weapon will form part of a collection (. . .)

Amendments:

Replace subsection 2.(4) of the bill with:

[The definition "restricted weapon" in subsection 84(1) of the said Act is amended by striking out the paragraph (c) thereof.]

Replace subsection 2.(2) of the bill with:

[Paragraph (c) of the definition "prohibited weapon" in subsection 84(1) of the said Act is repealed and the following substituted therefore: (c) any firearm that is capable of, or assembled or designed and manufactured with the capability of, firing projectiles in rapid succession during one pressure of the trigger, whether or not it has been altered to fire only one projectile with one such pressure,]

Delete subsection 20.(5) of the bill.

Purpose:

Require the Firearms Acquisition Certificate or equivalent for ammunition purchases.

As long as a gun owner needs ammunition for a legitimate purpose, said owner will have a FAC or an "equivalent," i.e. a hunting permit or the membership card of a shooting club. Collectors do not need ammunition. This provision would make it more difficult for an unlawful owner to purchase ammunition.

Means:

Add a subsection, similar to the one prohibiting the sale of firearms to anyone who does not have a FAC, with respect to ammunition and anyone without a FAC or equivalent.

Amendment:

Modify section 9 of the bill by adding the following subsection:

[9.(0) The first paragraph of subsection 97(1) of the said Act is replaced by the following: Everyone who sells, barters, gives, lends, transfers or delivers any firearm or ammunition to a person who does not, at the time of such a sale, barter, giving, lending, transfer or delivery or, in the case of a mail-order sale, within a reasonable time prior thereto, produce a Firearms Acquisition Certificate or, in the case of ammunition, a Firearms Acquisition Certificate or equivalent as prescribed by regulations, for inspection by the person selling, bartering, giving, lending, transferring or delivering the firearm or ammunition, that person has no reason to believe is invalid or was issued to a person other than the person producing it,]

It's fortunate that Jocelyne's office was equipped with more than one fax machine, for we made full use of the equipment in the early hours of that Monday morning. We sent a copy of the document to everyone who was involved in the gun-control debate, no matter whether they were committee members, reporters, justice officials or representatives of friendly groups. I took a pile of copies with me, ran home, changed into my "parliamentary" clothes, and hopped on the first bus to the capital.

Wendy, in the meantime, had written a letter of her own – and counselled other groups with theirs, even prodding them to have some of their members attend the proceedings. An hour before the opening statements, we handed all our documents to the chairman of the Justice Committee, Conservative MP Blaine Thacker. ("We thought you might be interested in this information, should the discussion turn to bypassing the hearings.")

We took our places in the committee room and listened to Kim Campbell's presentation. And yes, at the end of her remarks, she did argue that the committee should pass on further hearings:

"I would like to urge you to complete committee stage, if possible, before the House rises on Friday," she said. "I do believe there was extensive consultation on the subject, and my legislation is a response to that consultation. . . . I would very much like to see it move forward as quickly as possible. I have made no secret of my sense of urgency. I believe the people of this country would like to see action sooner rather than later."

Almost reluctantly, the chairman took her up on it. "Before we go on to questioning, I want to make a comment to the committee because it flows out of the minister's last bit of evidence. Over the weekend, I have had many groups contact me, as well as third parties, and there seems to be quite a broad basis of agreement that the previous bill was a very good proposal, but directed more to policy items. The current bill, flowing out of that, is a very good reflection of what went on, but there still are a number of proposals.

"Therefore, I think it is possible for this committee to hear witnesses on some technical matters without getting into the broad general policy. That is certainly my advice to you."

Campbell looked at the committee members, then at the reporters around her, all of whom had the student brief and the other letters in their hands.

Russell MacLellan, the spokesman for the Liberals, opined: "Our party, Mr. Chairman, is prepared to do so. We feel very strongly about it, to the extent that we are prepared to sit on this committee even after the summer adjournment begins, if that is what it's going to take. . . . Not everybody wants that opportunity, but certainly there are cases of people wishing to appear."

As if on cue, members of the National Action Committee on the Status of Women marched into the room through the big oak doors, shouting, "We are here as representatives of women across this country to tell you we want public hearings on gun control."

"We want women consulted!"

"We want public hearings!! We want public hearings!!"

It got so noisy, the chairman had no choice but to suspend the sitting for a few minutes and let the security guards clear the protesters away. But the message had gotten across.

That afternoon, the Legislative Committee decided to hold hearings in the fall.

11

"There is an automatic majority of FEMALES *who are not interested in male activities and who, for their convenience, simply suggest to ban it all, to squash all minorities. Brutal."*

– Sporting-goods distributor Nick Jerch

W endy and I were elated and, in what became a ritual of sorts whenever our work had a perceptible impact, we skipped and jumped to a nearby restaurant, chanting "We're so good" to no particular tune, and treated ourselves to victory milkshakes.

Granted, getting a bill delayed wasn't that great an accomplishment, but gave us an indication of our influence, and we felt positively lightheaded. We weren't watching from the sidelines anymore. We had reversed a minister's decision! We were so good!

It showed us the importance of dealing with individual MPs. Getting people to write to the prime minister had been a good idea but we knew that, for better results, our focus would have to move to the 294 other members of the House of Commons. They are the ones who debate their party's position, sit on committees, and vote on bills.

The question was, how could we reach every single MP? The very idea was overwhelming.

We had already tried to meet with a few after the last hearings. As we headed out of the parliamentary building, we noticed all these MP offices lining the corridors, and rationalized that as long as we were there we might as well make a couple more stops, knock on doors, hand out our leaflets.

Since we hadn't made appointments, most of our forays had ended with the secretaries in each office. We had managed to talk our way into meeting a few MPs, but we got a lot of funny looks in the bargain.

The guards caught up to us after our tenth attempt or so, and that brief lobbying manoeuvre ended with our being sternly escorted out of the building. Door-to-door soliciting, we were told, was strictly prohibited in the House.

(We hadn't really thought about it from the politicians' perspective! Parliament would be crawling with solicitors if anyone could drop in unannounced. It's a wonder we got as far as we did in the first place.)

The trouble was, our influence with the MPs paled beside that of their constituents. If we wanted politicians to support gun control, the pressure would have to come from within their ridings.

Time to get the locals involved.

❧

To convince the MPs to back the demands that we'd make during the upcoming hearings, we'd have to repeat what we had done with the mail-in campaign to the prime minister, only with 294 targets and much less help from the media. We had obtained a unique privilege when they published our form letter, but only because it tied the debacle of the bill to the massacre's anniversary.

Initially we didn't know what form the support we sought should take. Was it a bigger petition? People marching in the streets? Celebrities speaking out?

Just then, out of the blue, an Ottawa-area woman named Kathleen wrote to us to inquire about what she could do to help. She discussed it with Wendy for a while, and she decided to ask both her own and other town councils to endorse our position.

I must say I was baffled: I wasn't aware that town councils could do that, especially for an issue over which they had no jurisdiction. But why not? We wrote a sample letter. Kathleen did everything else.

What a surprise it was to learn, a few weeks later, that the City of Oakville was planning to organize a public meeting to discuss the issue. Wendy showed up to speak, but when she got there, the hall was crammed with gun users. Kathleen's parents seemed to be the only supporters in attendance!

Their intervention was all the more critical for it. They spoke very eloquently about the need to live in a safe environment, and in the end, despite all of our opponents' objections, the town did choose to endorse us. For these municipal councillors, the size of the crowd mattered less than the people's interest.

Wendy immediately saw the potential in this, and we

pursued more endorsements throughout the summer – not just from city councils, but from professional associations, health departments, peace groups, women's groups, churches, unions, colleges, universities. . . . We wrote hundreds of letters, following up with phone calls and visits in the case of the groups with the most influence.

The position we asked groups to endorse contained all of our demands, despite the fact that only a fraction of them were on the government's agenda. This way, the support of the groups would be valid until we obtained everything we considered necessary. In the long run, these endorsements were much more valuable than getting good press. Official support doesn't age; that's where a coalition gets its strength, not from quotes from last week's paper.

We eventually spoke for more than 350 organizations from the local to the national scale. At the time of the hearings, we could proudly state that we represented millions of citizens, not counting individual members. No matter how one added it up, that was a lot more support than the gun lobby could lay claim to.

Their contributions took many forms. A printer offered us free services. A Polytechnique administrator designed a data-base program adapted to our needs. And with her students' collaboration, a teacher from a secretarial school had our handwritten list of members' addresses entered on disks as part of a class project.

(There were others, however, who didn't quite understand our needs. Like that square-built man who spent over an hour waiting for me by the front desk and who showed a

huge serrated hunting knife to the terrified receptionists. He
left without explanation, and I never knew if he wanted to
offer protection or support stronger controls – for others
rather than himself, at least.)

But in most cases, we encouraged people to speak out in
one form of another.

One of our endorsers, the Church Council on Justice and
Corrections, had already orchestrated a "Don't kill for me"
postcard campaign, back when capital punishment was being
debated. We adapted the idea to our purpose. Jocelyne's
eight-year-old daughter Julia drew a picture of how she perceived gun control, and we had the artwork printed on cards,
with our demands on the back. Anyone could send a copy,
postage-free, to his or her MP.

That, in essence, was our second mail-in campaign. Once
again, we did innumerable interviews with journalists, and
Jocelyne picked up the tab for the printing and the postage.

Since there is no rule which says that people can write only
to their own MPs, we decided to ask a little more of the
callers. We found out who the key politicians were in each
province, and whenever supporters asked for a postcard, we
sent them twenty-five cards with the list of these MPs.

The campaign required a huge effort, with volunteers
taking over the office's conference room on every evening
and weekend. Each time the printer sent us five thousand
postcards, they had to be divided into packages of twenty-
five, matched with a list, bundled up, addressed, weighed and
stamped. Yet the piles of postcards never seemed to diminish,

as new shipments kept coming in all the time. I still get nau-
seated thinking about it.

Sending out so many cards was bound to have *some* effect
on the MPs, but measuring that impact was impossible. The
more obvious changes occurred at the grassroots level: a
silent majority was turned into a vocal one.

Which didn't prevent more than one MP from doubting
that they were the majority. This point had to be made so
often that Wendy finally got ticked off. When a Tory MP said
that we might learn something if we could see his riding, she
called him up and said, "Okay, we're coming."

And we did. As soon as we had enough for the air fare, we
packed our toothbrushes and booked two seats to the Far
West.

12

" 'What difference does it make whether you have a gun that can rapid-fire 17 bullets in a row or one that shoots one bullet at a time?' yelled one man. There was a ripple of laughter when someone said 15 minutes was all that was needed, no matter what kind of gun you had."

— Public meeting, Southam News account

Our Williams Lake hotel was charmingly rustic, a two-storey log cabin decked out with oil lamps and frontier memorabilia. I thought they were playing it up for the tourist trade, but then I caught a glimpse of the local bar, and it did feature swinging doors and men in cowboy hats.

I almost began expecting to see tough don't-mess-with-me gunslingers on every street corner.

I *know* that's a stereotype. But such misconceptions tainted both sides of the debate. Since the beginning, we've been called emotional strident hysterical uninformed dishonest misguided pie-in-the-sky absolutist Nazi baby-killing ghouls. This was the point of our trip out west: to build bridges, extend olive branches, tear down fences, and all that.

So far, things had gone relatively smoothly. Before we even set foot in Vancouver, our B.C. coordinator, Ray, had set up well over a dozen rendezvous, and offered to drive us from one to the next. We just let the whirlwind engulf us, and the meetings with reporters, mayors, and police chiefs blended into a blurry rush.

If I had ever thought that touring dignitaries had it easy, I now knew better. We never had a moment to ourselves, we kept repeating the same arguments from one meeting to the next, and we were always aware of precious minutes ticking away. It seemed that no sooner were we getting a charge out of a particular exchange, than we were forced to cut it short, hurry off to our next stop, and twiddle our thumbs in another waiting room. As far as roller-coaster rides went, this one grew more wearisome by the hour.

Nonetheless, meeting people face to face had been much more effective than phoning or writing. Personal contact increased people's interest, made our message clearer, and got us greater commitments. I still hadn't seen any difference with the way people treated us back home . . . but I was pretty sure that things would change once we had left the coast behind.

Williams Lake is a small town on the San Jose River, four hundred kilometres north of Vancouver, but much closer to the Albertan border than the Pacific Ocean. It's a ten-hour train ride from Vancouver, and aside from the Yukon, it felt as if there was no more remote place for a Montrealer like myself.

I spent most of the journey pressed up against the window, drinking in the spectacular landscape. This was my first visit to the Rockies and I found it absurd not to spend more time out there, rather than saving it for a verbal showdown about guns.

On the other hand, Conservative MP Dave Worthy was an influential member of the Legislative Committee. If we wanted him on our side, we would have to put on a good show.

In spite of the challenge he had given us, he was an amiable man who really went out of his way to make us feel welcome. Having always seen him in a business suit, I was surprised to discover how much more comfortable he seemed in jeans and a denim shirt. Ruggedly time-worn, with a square jaw and eyes ablaze, he looked like a retired cowboy. What's more, he genuinely had *both* the interests and the safety of his riding at heart. Which was a relief, as he would personally moderate the debate that night.

But first, we all headed towards the local radio station for a group interview.

Ever since we had landed, Wendy's role had been to present the experts' evidence and to introduce the solutions we were promoting. My part was more loosely defined, but no less important: I brought the statistics to life and bore witness that the ravages were not just an abstraction. *I was there* when my classmates were gunned down.

As with the Special Committee, my testimony doubled as a moderating factor. Aside from defining the stakes, it fostered sympathy, and made our opponents less inclined to attack us.

I do wish we could have dispensed with such symbols – gun control is a rational choice, not a sentimental one. But since I had needed a tragedy to get involved, I hardly could deny other people's desire to focus on the human dimension of the issue.

Over lunchtime, we ran a few errands – I got a new roll of film and Wendy bought a large-capacity magazine. She wanted to use it for show and tell. (The gun store didn't sell any assault weapons, by the way. As far as we could tell, they wouldn't mind their being banned.)

We spent the rest of the afternoon in meetings, with the head of the local RCMP detachment, and with a reporter from the local newspaper. But through it all, Wendy could see that the prospect of facing a roomful of defensive gun owners that evening had rattled me.

"You may want to tone down your testimony," she suggested. "Around here, talking at length about the massacre might be perceived as emotional blackmail."

I was only too glad to comply. This was one of those times where I would be perfectly content to sit back and take notes.

However, I was as determined as Wendy to show that we weren't against hunting or target practice, and we accepted an invitation to the local gun club so we could take a few shots out in their training field.

I had never used a gun before, and it took me some time to get used to the idea that I was able to kill by flexing my index finger! I suppose that this is not on a target shooter's mind all the time, but the thought was never far away from mine. To me, the danger starts when one sees a gun as an ordinary piece of equipment and forgets the risks intrinsic to all firearms.

Simply taking the shotgun in my hands made me realize how much trust is part of the activity. As long as I held the gun, everyone had to trust me; they had no choice. This wasn't too hard to do in this particular situation, nor would it be when well-acquainted people train together. But after everything I had learned in recent months, nobody could have convinced me to extend this principle to society at large.

My first shot, then, and it had to be in front of twenty reporters and experienced shooters! We were given a few safety tips, and I was surprised by how quickly the following minutes went by.

Each target consisted of a series of small silhouettes of animals at various distances down the field. We tried to shoot at half a dozen of them, one after the other, and the photographers went wild during the entire exercise.

Our final score: one out of three silhouettes on average, which we were told was quite honourable, considering our beginner status. The atmosphere warmed up, and I got to see firsthand how easy it was to forget about the social implications of guns when you're focussing on toppling little bunnies.

By 7 P.M., about forty people had shown up for the debate. Under the placid gaze of the room's hunting trophies, our host introduced us, and from then on, Wendy virtually took charge of the evening. Confident and knowledgeable, she segued effortlessly from one point to the next, phrasing her arguments in positive terms and rebutting objections before they could be raised. When she got around to talking about training and safe storage, she had the whole audience agreeing with her. They didn't care for recklessness any more than we did.

Although the tone remained civilized throughout the

entire evening, some antagonism did surface when the floor was opened for questions.

"You can't just come in here and tell us what to do," was the gist of what they said. "What do you know about our way of life?"

Very patiently, Wendy explained that we were not asking for a ban on hunting rifles, only for a registry that would help prevent misuses. Wasn't that reasonable enough?

"But that's only a problem in big cities! Why punish *us* for it?"

"You should feel just as concerned. Many studies were made about this, and they all conclude that, other things being equal, guns kill more people in rural areas."

"Are you saying that we are less respectful of the law than city folks?"

"Not at all. We're talking about a very simple equation: where there are more guns, there are more gun deaths."

"It's not that black and white. I work on search-and-rescue missions, and I find a Ruger with a folding stock mighty useful in a confined helicopter cabin. . . ."

"Maybe so, but that's an exceptional circumstance. It doesn't justify treating all military weapons like ordinary shotguns."

"It's the reverse we're afraid of. Once we register our rifles, you might call for their confiscation, leaving us with no guns at all!"

"That's an unfounded fear. Cars and dogs have been registered for a long time, and *they* haven't been banned. The idea is not to question whether you can own guns, it's whether you can keep it a secret."

"That may be true, but the government already has its nose in too much of our business. Why should we let the pencil-pushers invade our privacy like that?"

Had the point been to win people over, we'd have failed miserably. As reassuring as we tried to be, we couldn't have reversed ingrained convictions in less than two hours.

But that wasn't all we were there for. We were also playing to the bigger audience, the one represented by the journalists sitting in the back row.

As of that day, our views would be more accurately perceived by both the public and the media – and Dave Worthy would have less reason to believe that all his constituents were opposed to gun control.

⁂

So much for being ridden out of town in a tar-and-feather outfit. We were well treated in most of the places we visited – Calgary, Red Deer, Winnipeg, among others – but not everywhere. When she made further trips by herself, Wendy did encounter a lot more resistance, which wasn't helped by moderators who "proved to be ineptness personified," to use one journalist's assessment.

Then again, people had more trouble understanding her motivation. Whether or not they agreed with me, gun owners knew where I was coming from, while few could accept the same commitment in someone who hadn't been affected by the massacre in a personal way. A city-dwelling, secure woman who acted out of pure idealism, Wendy must have seemed like an antichrist to them, and they made no bones about sharing that feeling with her.

Many audiences yelled at her non-stop, heaping abuse on each and every one of her points and making the organizers fear for her safety.

One crowd actually cheered when a police video she was showing stated that a semi-automatic weapon could "turn a peaceful neighbourhood into a war zone." "Right on," a voice shouted to gales of laughter. More than once, gun owners publicly threatened to register their guns in Wendy's name, and if a member of the audience expressed her fear of confronting an armed assailant, she was immediately told to "buy a gun" herself.

Unintimidated, Wendy let it all fly past her. When anyone stood up to speak in her defence, she'd always feel deeply grateful, but if no one rose from the sea of screaming faces, she would fend for herself, sometimes staying in combat mode for days on end.

It took its toll though: she sometimes had trouble readjusting to normal life. The stress made it hard to switch tracks for some quiet time with her family.

She had to keep reminding herself that, as draining and depressing as these events might be, they might galvanize the people who heard about them into doing something. All she needed was one columnist or editorialist to take her side.

PUBLIC TOO SILENT ON GUN CONTROL, admonished one headline after a particularly ugly evening in Edmonton. "Wendy," the paper said, "must have felt completely alone in a city of 600,000. . . . Where were you when it really counted?"

Whenever we got good coverage of these events, the mail would flow in to our office. Sometimes, even our opponents' greatest efforts were winning us more support.

13

"If I lost my large-capacity magazines, I could no longer compete because changing magazines every five rounds is difficult and painful for me because I suffer from arthritis."
– Edith Iwawa, target shooter, to Legislative Committee

I'm never in the dream. I don't have to be. Imagining what happened to the girls is as horrible as it can get. They're engineering students, sitting in the chairs I sat in, with the same problems on their minds. They *are* me.

They're all doing their thing, eating, talking, planning their evening, and reviewing their notes. The cafeteria is abuzz with excitement and laughter. When the man with the gun walks in, no one spots him right away.

He looks around, in no particular rush – he seems very sure of himself. One girl does turn and take notice, unsure of what she should make of him. She whispers something to a friend. A few more heads look up –

He starts shooting. I merge with the students about whom I've heard the most, like the two who had just enough time to huddle together before they were killed. I try to find an exit, a secret passage, something to ward off the bullets, and I realize that there's no escape. It's now too clear, too precise, too real: I shiver, twitch, and jolt, and my eyes fly wide open, averting the end of the scene.

I'll toss and turn for a long time before I can switch to different thoughts. Until then, there's no way I'll let my defences down again.

᠅

Stepping back into the office after our sojourn felt like walking into pure frenzy. My desk was overflowing with urgent messages, and boxes of paperwork were edging into the passageways, piling up in the conference room, even waiting in the reception area. Requests for postcards alone would keep our volunteers busy for many long nights.

Then, in the fall of 1991, a strike shut down the postal system, and our workload went from heavy to nightmarish. We tried to work around it with couriers, but it was rough on our dwindling finances. We had nothing left for unexpected emergencies. All we could do was wait for a little breather, anything that would let us recoup from the blows.

And so, of course, came the next crisis.

"There's a problem with the hearings," Wendy said on the phone, on the last Wednesday in September.

We were both about to leave for Ottawa, and, for a change, we were both well prepared. Over the summer, we had worked hard to make sure the committee members would be as open as possible to our demands. Since I was scheduled to testify the next day, the last thing I wanted to hear was that something had gone awry.

"What now?"

"I just got a call from the Hill. Seems that the Tory MPs who oppose the bill have managed to get the party whip on side."

(The whip is the man in charge of party discipline: among other things, he selects the committee members for his party. Jim Hawkes, the Conservative whip, was from the heart of Alberta.)

"Oh, hell! Can he affect the outcome of the hearings?" I asked.

"Can and will. He's just reassigned most of the committee members who may have been favourable to us and replaced them with his cronies."

I was petrified. This could mean that the gun lobby would be welcomed with open arms, and our demands would be completely ignored. By the end of the hearing, the bill would be watered down to nothing.

To think that the bill had nearly sailed through three months earlier! We could spin it any way we wanted, but if we hadn't intervened, the legislation wouldn't be in jeopardy today.

"Why, it's outright sabotage! Can't Campbell fight back?"

"Her hands are tied – it's all been done by the book, and the party would never tolerate it if she aired its dirty laundry in public. If we don't want the bill to be emptied of all meaning, *we* will have to fight the whip, and quick."

❧

The letter we faxed to our supporters was an attention-grabber:

THE GUN CONTROL BILL MAY BE SCUTTLED!
At this very moment, a single man's efforts may be destroying everything we've done for gun control.

The government whip, Jim Hawkes, has recently asked pro-gun advocates to replace the Conservative MPs he had originally chosen for the study of the new bill. He has also nominated himself on the committee, a highly unusual move which will very likely endanger the fairness of the hearings, especially since he has openly admitted that he opposes gun control.

Only one of the nine members has spoken out in favour of gun control. The rest of the committee over-represents western and rural areas, while under-representing women and urban interests. We suspect that this small group will gut the bill of all significance in order to be re-elected in constituencies where gun interests run high.

Therefore, we urge you to phone or fax the following key MPs as soon as possible. Insist on the necessity of a balanced committee. Tell them it's unacceptable to dilute the already weak bill any further, and call for stricter improvements instead.

Be direct and act speedily. By next Wednesday, the bill may have become a shadow of its former self.

We sent out a similar message in a press release on the following Friday – a bad day to get the attention of the media, who are winding down for the weekend. This Friday was no different and precious few reporters paid us any attention. Even worse, the country was in the midst of a debate over constitutional reform, and it tied up most political reporters and blocked out the other issues. All we were promised was that our release would be handed to the news editor on Monday morning.

Such a weak commitment was of little comfort to us, so we asked some of our individual supporters to phone the media as well and protest their poor coverage of the hearings.

It seemed like a lost cause. Getting anyone to make a phone call was never easy, especially when it was about such a complex matter and on such short notice. Few of them believed that their complaints would have any effect anyway. Yet this was precisely why we had to try: individuals speak out so rarely that those who do are assumed to represent a much larger audience.

Once again, we ran our volunteers ragged all weekend. The previous spring's push before the hearings was put to shame in all respects. Come Monday morning, I didn't have to take a bus to the capital – I was still stationed there. And I was as ready as I could be for a meeting with the Tory whip.

❧

He rose and shook my hand, but that's as far as the pleasantries went. We both knew we stood on opposite sides, and we had little interest in meaningless banter.

I started in, "Thank you for seeing me on such short notice. As you know, the new composition of the Legislative Committee is troubling us . . ."

I kept my voice calm, free of any accusation. Regardless of what I believed, I couldn't express the anger that I felt.

He smiled and nodded faintly through my analysis of the situation. A consummate politician, he was the type of man I couldn't imagine without a suit and tie. When he finally spoke, his tone was as courteous as my own, but there was a mischievous glint in his eye.

It's a shame I thought there was a bias, he said, taking time to weigh every one of his words. He had never had questionable intentions: the original list of committee members was several months old, and I shouldn't find it disconcerting that it had been updated.

"But you can't deny that the present line-up is heavily weighted in favour of western and rural concerns . . ."

He waved the objection away. All he had done was choose members who were more knowledgeable about guns.

"You think that gun control should be left to gun *owners*?"

Of course, he replied. Gun owners, of all people, are most interested in gun safety. After all, isn't it in their interest to prevent hunting accidents? He said he found the proposals and statistics of the hunting organizations to be the most reliable ones he had seen.

How naïve did he think I was? He *must* have known that the gun lobby, as a whole, cared less about public-safety issues than about avoiding more fees and red tape. The true experts in crime prevention and public health are those whose job it is to protect the public – doctors and police officers – the same people who, every day, experience firsthand the consequences of the misuse of guns. Yet he was telling me that their views were less worthy, even irrelevant?

We argued a little longer, but I realized that it wouldn't make one bit of difference. When he looked at me, he saw a very young woman, a fresh-out-of-school graduate who couldn't possibly be a threat to him. All he had to do was placate me, saying, There, there, I've sat down and listened to you. Now you can leave and stop making a fuss.

I got up. "I guess I won't persuade you, but I had to inform you about our feelings. I hope you realize that we won't take it sitting down."

Again, he smiled, as if to say, *Go ahead, do your worst. See if I care.*

ॐ

In my presence Hawkes had been very careful not to tip his hand as to any dubious intent.

But he did say some alarming things, and relaying my recollections of them to journalists wouldn't be a breach of secrecy – unless specified otherwise, anything an MP says in a meeting is on the record.

Wendy, in the meantime, had made rounds of calls to friendly politicians of all parties, urging them to speak out against the trap that had been laid out for the bill. Our non-partisan approach paid off: not only were opposition MPs prepared to condemn the whip's hidden agenda, but Barbara

Greene – one of Hawkes' own colleagues – agreed to break rank and denounce what he had done.

We hastily called a press conference for the following morning, and once under way, we didn't have to make any accusations ourselves. We just stated the facts about the committee's composition, I recounted parts of my conversation with Hawkes and the MPs we introduced were the ones who cried foul play.

The media finally showed interest, rapidly spreading the news through midday radio and television broadcasts. When Wendy made her afternoon appearance before the committee on behalf of the Coalition, Hawkes had visibly lost his composure. Instead of questioning her about her presentation, he used all of his allotted time to defend his actions.

"I gather you had a press conference today. You put up a press release, and you had questions for me. I was not warned about them, and was not in a position to answer them."

Wendy didn't bat an eyelash. "Actually," she said, "Heidi Rathjen had a meeting with you on Monday, and did put the questions to you, so it was not completely from outer space...."

She then repeated all of our concerns about the committee's membership, thereby entering them in the parliamentary record. If anyone in the audience hadn't known about the last-minute replacements, this brought them up to speed in the most official way.

Hawkes floundered. He went on to assure us that he was "a human being" and had been "a university professor with a Ph.D. in psychology" with "a reasonable record of being concerned about people." The next day, even the Western papers were full of "stacked the Commons committee" and "sabo-taged gun-control legislation."

The prime minister was forced to step in. When Mulroney spoke to party members during the next day's caucus meeting, he told Hawkes and his allies to back off, and later promised in media interviews that none of the amendments would be "offensive to the parents who had their daughters massacred."

His statements left no room for discussion. When the committee reported back to the House, the bill was even stronger than it had been going in.

Victory milkshakes all round!

14

"My cousin was shot with a shotgun. The killer was aiming at someone else but the bullets went right through him and killed my cousin. . . . I am certain that he would be alive today if handguns were more readily available."

— Michael Martinoff, National Firearms Association
legal-affairs expert, to the Senate Committee

The improvements the committee recommended were significant. They included raising the age to obtain a Firearms Acquisition Certificate from sixteen to eighteen, requiring a photograph on the FAC, and shifting the burden of proof onto the applicant as opposed to the officer when one is refused.

Once the Legislative Committee handed the bill back to the House of Commons for the third reading, there was little more we could do. If the House accepted the report as a whole, as it usually does, we'd be reasonably satisfied . . . for the time being.

Yet the controversy hadn't abated. The MPs were still feeling fierce pressure in their ridings from both camps, and very few cared to go on the record for either side.

So they wimped out. The major parties agreed on a motion to pass the bill without a registered vote. This way, the individual MPs would not have to choose sides: no vote would be recorded, and no private loyalties would be revealed. If any of them feared reprisals from the gun lobby for having let the bill go through, they could always say that they *would* have voted against it, but they never had the chance.

The scheme might have worked if we hadn't decided that we really wanted a registered vote. Politicians, we believed, had a duty to take a public stand, and be held accountable for it. Moreover, we knew the battle for gun control wouldn't end with this bill, and we wanted to know everyone's position for future reference.

The rules of the House state that it only takes six MPs to force a registered vote. So we asked the members of the Bloc Québécois to hang in until the end of the debate and do just that. Securing their collaboration was a snap: not only did they support gun control, but they had so often been reduced to passive observers by the other parties that they leapt at the chance to derail their opponents' plan.

What followed soon degenerated into low comedy. When the word got around that a registered vote might still be in the cards, the Tories and the Liberals resolved to stall the proceedings. One after another, their back-benchers were sent in to give deadly *dull*, protracted speeches, in the hopes that the Bloc members would give up and leave.

"As young guys," droned the MP from Fraser West Valley, "we would get a bunch of cans and put them up on those long, endless fences that stretch across for miles and miles, as far as you can see, and each try and make a few shots at them. You learn something from that about being Canadian, about being free, about having space." And so on.

Our allies bravely held their ground. After checking his son into a hospital, one of them even flew back in to sit through this drivel late into the night.

The motion to hold an unregistered vote was defeated at eight minutes past midnight when it became clear that their delaying tactics were going nowhere. The legislation was voted through later that day, and everyone's position was noted in the parliamentary record.

≫

The bill went on to the Senate.

We were now in the last days of November 1991, and the impending break in parliamentary activities made us extremely nervous: word on the Hill was, the prime minister would end the parliamentary session right after the holidays, effectively killing Bill C-17, along with all other bills that had not reached the end of the legislative process.

I couldn't predict what would happen to the bill in the Senate. Not being elected, senators were less affected than the House by the opinion of voters (or the pressure of lobby groups). But they also didn't like being rushed. The Senate's role as a place of sober second thought had often been ridiculed, and they were quite sensitive about the value of their deliberations. No matter how pressed for time, they wouldn't approve a bill without at least the semblance of a proper review.

They still had three weeks before the holidays, but that isn't much in the world of politics. Could thorough consultations and analyses fit into such a short period?

The first indication of the senators' inclination came when they announced how much time they were reserving for their committee hearings on the bill – one day for our side, and one day for the gun groups. Hardly any time at all. It almost sounded as if . . . *they were trying to finish the job by December 6!* They wouldn't have rushed the process to deliver bad news on the day of the anniversary, now, would they?

A second sign of their goodwill was the cordial atmosphere in which these hearings were conducted. The senators' questions were smart, respectful, and on target. It almost struck me dumb: in my brief career on Parliament Hill, this was the first government panel I had encountered that consistently approached the issue in terms of public safety, rather than the private interests of a minority. For once, it was the gun lobby that was on trial, not us.

Unlike the Special Committee that had pored over the first bill, the Senate committee welcomed testimonies from the families of gun victims. Suzanne volunteered once more for the task, and this time she was joined by three other witnesses, John Bickerstaff, Eric Sirois, and Priscilla De Villiers.

John's son Lee was with five other teenagers at his best friend's place when they found a revolver. Fascinated by the weapon, they got into a game of Russian roulette. Lee lost. A gun owner himself, John asked his friends and relatives to make a donation to the Coalition instead of sending flowers to Lee's funeral, and he soon became one of our most fervent supporters.

Eric was so distressed after an accident with the family car that he grabbed his father's hunting rifle and shot himself in the mouth. Miraculously, he survived – but the bullet left him blind. He wanted his story to be known, and he also spoke on behalf of all people whose temporary depression had led to their death because of a gun.

Priscilla lost her daughter at the hands of a psychopath. Out on parole after an eleven-year string of violent crimes, the killer legally owned a rifle, as there was no system to flag such aberrations. After sexually assaulting a woman in Ontario and murdering another in New Brunswick, he shot Nina, then took his own life.

A senseless massacre, a deadly game, a temporary bout of despair, a fatal abduction – together, these stories painted a devastating portrait of firearms unchecked. Had long guns been registered, the inquest into Nina's murder found, both her death and the New Brunswick woman's might have been averted. Yet the bill didn't even go that far. Even so, our opponents were calling it draconian!

The senators got the message. Many of them came to us in private after our presentation and asked us if we really wanted them to pass this mediocre package. Wouldn't we rather hold out for a more complete bill?

They had a point. We knew that once the law was adopted, the issue of gun control was unlikely to remain in the public eye long enough for us to push for stronger measures. But the whip's attempted coup had spooked us. An all-or-nothing attitude might just leave us empty-handed. It wasn't a risk we cared to take. This bill could save more lives than were lost in the massacre.

So we said no, vote it through. Batten down the minimum, but recommend the registration of all guns, the ban on assault weapons, and everything that's still missing. Write an open letter to Kim Campbell. Let the whole country know that this is not enough.

And they did. Incomplete as it was, the legislation was passed by the Senate on the evening of December 5, 1991, after resounding speeches praising our work and honouring the victims. Since she had too often been replaced by a substitute already, Wendy had to leave Ottawa immediately afterwards for a class she was teaching back in Toronto, but I stayed behind to make sure everyone knew that we saw this as just the beginning.

I could barely contain myself – I was thinking of all those people who didn't want the victims to have died in vain. A few hours later, that was exactly what all the news bulletins were saying about the December 6 tragedy.

YEARS THREE TO SIX

15

"When you look back on this Christmas, you'll be delighted with the oohs and aahs as your family and friends opened their unique gifts. . . . But more important, you'll remember that you bought so much more than just gifts. That's because, with every purchase from this catalogue, you're also helping to support the many vital projects that [we] undertake."

– Plush toy promotion, Canadian Wildlife Federation
(a gun-lobby group)

If this were a movie, the story would probably end here. A tragedy takes place, a social wrong is revealed, a battle ensues, and virtue triumphs. Fade out.

Real life, however, isn't so neat.

Oh, for the next month or so, Wendy and I had a spring in our walk and a perpetual smile on our faces. The sense of achievement was fabulous, and we couldn't wait to celebrate with all of our supporters, from the MPs who had risked their necks to everyone who had ever worked on our mailings.

We didn't have much money for a celebration, so we settled for homemade snacks and cheap bubbly over at Kathleen's. We covered a wall with editorial cartoons that had poked fun at the gun lobby, and the festivities just took off from there.

Most people hadn't met each other before, and the conversations were peppered with "So *you're* the one who . . ." and

"I didn't get to thank you for . . ." Until then, I had never been in the company of so many supporters – and in a celebratory mood, no less! The energy level was sky high; it was a true reward for all those months of work. We let our hair down, raised our glasses, and basked in the warm, safe embrace of our partners' and friends' congratulations.

❧

Joanne

I know Heidi thinks I'm exaggerating but, for me, there's no other way to put it: the Coalition saved my life.

Back when I was living with my uncle in 1982, I too faced the dark barrel of a gun. We were temporarily sheltering a homeless man, and after I had spent an arduous day cleaning up the place, I sternly asked him to take his socks off the dinner table. His only response was to pull out a revolver and fire two shots at the wall next to me.

I tried to hide my fear. Without taking my eyes off him, I slowly backed into the kitchen to phone the police. But before I had a chance to say anything, he burst into the room, the gun now squarely aimed at my forehead. He pulled the trigger twice, but only hit empty chambers. I leapt towards the door, and a third shot flattened me against the fridge.

I regained consciousness in the ambulance, with a punctured lung and a bullet pressing on my spinal cord. I went through four major operations in a row and, since neither of my parents could take care of me, I was left to fend for myself. Constant pain and acute anxiety prevented me from earning a stable living, so I moved into a tiny apartment and began a long struggle to receive proper treatments.

I was nineteen years old and I felt as if my life was over.

When I came across an article about Heidi, it was like a revelation. Transforming my misfortune into a cause I cared about had never occurred to me. Since I had some experience with computers, I offered her my help, yet I believe it's my personal story that compelled her to take me on, one day a week or so. No matter what contributions I may have made, I'm sure that I'm the one who benefited the most from our time together.

Whether I was stuffing envelopes or meeting with my MP, doing something about guns was a way to fight against the violence that had shattered my life. And instead of complaining away, the way I used to, I learned how to channel my frustrations in a more constructive fashion. I even founded my own organization to defend the rights of crime victims!

If there's one thing I wish on other survivors, it's that they find a way to arrive at the same sense of dignity that the Coalition has instilled in me.

⁂

Then a few days later, I was laid off.

It didn't came as a surprise – Jocelyne had hired me only for six months. When the deadline was reached in the middle

of the House hearings, she had kindly extended our arrangement for another three months, but now that the law had
been passed, she'd have to let me go. My only option was to
stay there and continue my work without pay. But that
cubicle was beginning to feel cramped. If I was to carry on, I
would have to get a bigger office.

When I told Jocelyne I'd be moving on, she was truly sad-
dened – but a little relieved too. She had sacrificed a lot for me.

For a while I considered moving everything to my apartment, but that would have meant forfeiting my last square
metre of free space. When I mentioned my predicament to
public-health officials, one of them told me there were a few
vacant offices in the public-health department of the Sainte-
Justine Children's Hospital. He made some calls, and they
agreed to let me use one of them for free.

It was a tiny room, but it was three times the size my
cubicle had been. We put in a desk, two filing cabinets, a
couple of shelves, and a photocopier – that was more than
enough. Best of all, I now had my very own door, so there was
no more dress code. I could wear running shoes to work as
often as I wanted.

Better still, the department agreed to pay for my postage
and long-distance calls, and hired me to work on a research
contract about kids and guns. It allowed me carry on my
usual gun-control duties until the Coalition had received
enough donations to cover a decent salary.

All told, my working conditions had noticeably improved
. . . but for what purpose?

I tend to refer to the 1992–1993 period as "the boring

years," but it's a misnomer. Wendy and I never stopped working ten- to twelve-hour days, six to seven days a week. If a press release could be improved, or if I still had a few more calls to return, the hour I wanted to spend at the gym quickly lost its importance. *After all*, the back of my mind would whisper, *this is about saving lives.*

Come to think about it, I'm amazed that neither of us burned out.

The time that Wendy set aside to be with her daughter must have been her reprieve. As for me, I made it a point to disconnect as soon as I left the office. I'd *plan* to take a few days off at my parents' place in the countryside. Their property is a true sanctuary, dominated by a large willow that leans over a stream, and with tall pine trees all around. The mere idea of spending time away from my files, my phone, and my computer was enough to refresh me.

Whenever they came to see me in Montreal, my dad would pretend to believe my eager promise to visit, and my mom would smile an understanding smile, but they were well aware that it wasn't going to happen anytime soon. The all-encompassing push for the bill had now given way to a long stretch of small crises, one after another in tight formation.

ॐ

First, we had to watch over the regulations: a bill is skeletal law; once adopted, it has to be fleshed out with details and procedures. This process determines its ultimate strength – or deprives it of any bite.

Among other things, "safe storage" still had to be defined, as well as figuring out who could act as a reference and what would appear on the application form. As usual, the government would try to steer clear of anything too difficult or controversial. So we warned the press of potential concessions (February), reacted to the proposals (March), denounced an attempt to weaken them (June), responded to the final product (July), and protested against implementation delays (December).

A second issue we followed was the exemptions: the bill as it stood allowed provincial governments to exempt certain shooting competitions from the ban on large-capacity magazines. We were prepared to accept limited exceptions for recognized Olympic-class events, but we didn't want them to be so broad that they could apply to private war games.

We put in regular calls to the chief firearms officer in each province, trying to find out when they would address the issue. "Not yet," they kept saying – until we were tipped off that the Nova Scotia Department of Justice had just proclaimed their guidelines, two days earlier. Sure enough, many gun clubs had already been exempted, and some of them *did* organize military simulations.

We went into overdrive and faxed this information to anyone in the province who might feel concerned. We soon discovered that Halifax police chief Vincent MacDonald himself hadn't been notified, even though his own staff had started granting the exemptions!

When we told him about it, he flew into a blue rage.

Storming into the Permits Department, he put an immediate stop to the practice. Then he turned around and publicly notified the provincial justice minister that his office wouldn't authorize *any* exemption.

The media went to town with the story, and everyone applauded his position. Claiming that there had been a clerical error, the minister reversed his decision and denied he had ever supported the exemptions.

Moving quickly, we sent an overview of the scandal to all the other provincial justice ministers, and within a few weeks, even the gun-friendly provinces adopted a "no exemption" policy.

Then there were the Supreme Court rulings. No matter what the laws say, there will always be people who try to have them struck down by the courts, most often by appealing the verdict in a related case. This takes an enormous amount of time. Appeals slowly work through the courts, but it's the Federal Supreme Court that has the final say. The judgments about guns that were coming from the highest court referred to the *previous* law, adopted thirteen years before.

In one instance, a collector argued that the ban on automatic weapons did not cover semi-automatics such as his own Uzi, which could easily be *converted* to an automatic. The Supreme Court disagreed, and it did not mince words in condemning the civilian use of firearms that were designed for killing large numbers of people. The statement did a lot to reinforce our call for a ban on all paramilitary weapons.

A second defendant objected to the section of the law which forbade the use or storage of guns "without reasonable precautions for the safety of other people." This, he argued, violated his freedom. Again, the Supreme Court judges disagreed, and we had a field day with the outcome.

Lower court cases were also a concern: new trials were sprouting up all over, but they were not always cause for celebration.

For instance, when a Quebec gun merchant pleaded guilty to illegal firearm sales and falsely reporting the theft of forty weapons, he lost his permit to sell guns. When his son applied for one so that he could take over the business, the police argued that his father would still own the premises, finance the operations and, in all likelihood, run the show. They turned him down. He took them to court.

It should have been an open-and-shut case. According to the law, the police can turn down an applicant if they have reasonable grounds to think that there *might* be a security risk. But the judge looked no further than the son's credentials. Since his record was clean, the permit was granted.

The Crown neglected to appeal. The two men stayed in business.

Getting good press was a priority. One way or another, we had to keep the debate alive, in order to strengthen public support and keep the government from ignoring us.

It was a scattershot approach: we sent out releases, we organized media events. Whether we got covered or not, we kept on trying. At times, the only reason for doing so was to show we weren't going away: when several groups within a given area or profession were prepared to take a public stand, we'd organize a press conference around their support.

It was the tour all over again – Wendy or I would fly in to arouse media interest. We'd meet with everyone an hour before starting time, review the presentations, and try out tough questions to make sure everyone had mastered the subject. If need be, they could refer the queries to us – or we could jump in and complete what they had said.

We also hooked onto the news items which pertained to the law – or, more accurately, to its weaknesses. Despite the recent changes, the occasions weren't scarce.

For example, when the public was relieved to learn that a shipment of thousands of AK-47s had been stopped at the New York border, we had to stress that these firearms were in fact *legal* in Canada, and that the delivery had only been blocked because of improperly filled forms. Assault weapons were banned in other countries, we pointed out, that's why they were being redirected here by a specialized distribution network.

Cases of gun-related crimes also reinforced our position: not *all* "law-abiding" gun owners are as responsible as the gun lobby claimed they are.

There was this gun club member who killed four people before committing suicide. There was this gun collector who killed his neighbour for criticizing his lack of maturity. There was this gun merchant and white supremacist who killed a local trapper. There was this legally blind security guard who killed someone during a fight. There was this shooting instructor who caused the death of his eight-year-old stepson while teaching him to fire a .44 Magnum.

Each of these tragedies would deserve a chapter of their own if they didn't occur every day. That's a predicament we faced: so many lives are cut short by gunfire that it takes something much more spectacular to shock everyone out of their complacency.

The December 6 massacre did this to us.

And two years later, on August 24, 1992, it happened again.

16

"I pledge to defend, with my life if necessary, my right to own firearms. . . . I pledge to stockpile ammunition, firearms and reloading supplies in a safe place for my future use in case of invasion, civil unrest or government oppression."

– Gun Owners' Pledge, Access to Firearms'
Web site, Whitehorse, Yukon

Just this once, I had left work early. I usually couldn't. In addition to my other tasks, I handled the documentation centre of the Coalition, and I was always sifting through letters, transcripts, reports, statistics, releases, briefs, studies, speeches, clippings, forms, memos, bulletins, and files of all our activities. When there wasn't a crisis forcing me to stack them in one big pile in an attempt to clear the decks, I had to find a home for each document if I wanted to be able to unearth it later. It took time.

But on that day, I had managed to do everything by 4:30 P.M. – a rare achievement. Our newsletter was still two months behind schedule, but I felt so good about all the filing I'd done and the space I'd cleared, I decided not to mess it up until the next morning.

I locked up, strapped on my Rollerblades, and skated home. By the time I walked in, I had slipped into off-duty mode, and was looking forward to a night at the movies. I brought in a few groceries and put away my lunch containers. I checked my messages and heard "Heidi, turn the radio on, right now. There's been *another* mass shooting!"

The next thing I knew, I was hailing a cab back to the office.

❧

The story had a familiar ring to it. Man gets angry, man gets gun, man kills co-workers.

Like the first massacre, the shooting seemed to be a work of a "madman," with innocent people being attacked in broad daylight. The four men who were gunned down left their wives and eleven sons and daughters behind, not to mention other relatives and friends.

But the scale of the killings wasn't the only reason the media paid attention. Of all places, this had happened in another engineering department, at Concordia University, just minutes from the École Polytechnique.

The media would be out for blood. It wasn't the first time that professor Valery Fabrikant had accused the administration of conspiring against him. He had even talked of settling the situation "the American way." Since all of our campaigns had been about prevention, we'd be expected to issue vitriolic condemnations.

The phone *was* ringing when I ran in – it was Wendy, calling from a police conference she'd been attending. She had just heard about the murders.

"So what happened when the cops showed up?" she asked.

"They didn't say much. Seems the shooter surrendered without a fight."

"Any information on the weapon?"

"At least one handgun. Don't know how he got it."

"Try to find out more. I'll start working on a release, tie it in with general accessibility."

"Don't forget the permits. They're still too easy to get."

"Right. Call you back."

I listened to the other messages before digging up the phone numbers of my police contacts.

☙

"To legally acquire a handgun, one only needs to be the member of a gun club, be a gun collector or require it for employment. Once issued, there is no renewal process. The permit is valid for life, even if the initial reason for owning the gun ceases to exist. No follow-up of the owner is conducted to reassess his or her need for a concealable firearm. Permits for restricted weapons are free."
– Excerpt from the Coalition's press release, August 24, 1992.

Contrary to popular belief, the Sûreté had done everything it could under the law. But with so little control over who can own a handgun, and no systematic investigation of every applicant, there wasn't much they could have acted on.

Coming up with such a cold-hearted analysis wasn't easy. So many people expected an emotional response from me that I sometimes felt guilty for having hardened myself over the years. I suppose it's the same for doctors and police officers; you can't let every tragedy affect you while you're on duty.

Of course, I still feel anguish when I hear about a particularly gruesome incident. But the only times I never fail to agonize are when I meet a victim's spouse or parent. Their loss is direct, enormous, and permanent – and their distress is palpable. Even the most thorough news account cannot come close to the effect of spending five minutes with a grieving parent. Whenever Michèle Lemay tells me what my friendship meant to her Anne-Marie, I always go to pieces.

It wasn't like that with Mark Hogben, who approached the Coalition a few weeks after the shootings at Concordia. His father had been one of the teachers killed, and he was eager to help. He could have worked on any of the tasks the other volunteers handled, but to our good fortune, he offered to speak out about his loss.

We knew without a doubt that his testimony would have a striking effect on any audience. And yet, I hesitated.

"You may not realize how difficult this will be. You'll have to expose your pain to the entire country," I warned him.

"I know that. It will reopen the wounds every time. But I have to do it."

"Why?"

"Because gun control is a cause my father believed in. And he wouldn't have wanted me to wallow in self-pity. Whenever tragedy struck, he always said that something constructive should come out of it."

"Have you discussed this with your family?"

"Yes. They don't feel they can do much themselves, but we agreed that if I was up to it, then I should do whatever it takes."

This was great, but what should his specific position on the issue be?

Evidently, the university wanted to get rid of handguns. Within days of the attack, they had launched a petition calling for their total ban.

They asked for our endorsement, but our mandate didn't include a total ban on handguns, only tighter restrictions. When we had launched the Coalition, we had had to achieve a consensus among the most important health and safety organizations, and a handgun ban was going too far for some of them. We couldn't just add it to our platform without jeopardizing our support base.

On the other hand, Concordia had always been one of our strongest supporters, and we didn't want to offend them by rejecting their request. It was entirely legitimate to question the use of handguns in a civilized society, but we were already struggling just to ban assault weapons.

We could have asked our members to vote on it, but the risk of a rift was too great, and we didn't want to get bogged down in perpetual consultations. Besides, our opponents had long been saying that we were secretly seeking more restrictions than we admitted to. This was just the kind of thing that would have fuelled their argument.

After much deliberation, we decided to stay the course, and explained our position to the rector of Concordia and his team.

They were very understanding. They continued to support our work, and they promoted their initiative as a separate campaign. We encouraged our members to endorse their petition, and supporters of the university petition were told to join our coalition if they wanted more measures than just a ban on handguns.

Mark decided to back both positions, and became a marvellous speaker. He was genuine, level-headed, personable, and he never got sidetracked. No matter how difficult a question was, he would find answers that went straight to the heart of the matter.

All in the nick of time, too. Federal elections were coming, and the shootings at Concordia would put gun control front and centre on the political agenda.

17

"Gun owners are now the only white minority in the world."

– Chris Kingston, president, Restigouche Gun Club

At least, that's what I *thought* would happen.

Two horrifying massacres, two years apart from each other. Two massive public outcries for government action. You'd think it would be an obvious choice for any politician in search of a popular campaign promise.

You'd be wrong.

Despite our repeated attempts to keep gun control in the public eye, the clamour for further reforms had all but disappeared by the time the federal elections were called in the fall of 1993. The usual concerns about more jobs and less taxes were back at the forefront, and all the candidates acted as if the problem of firearms had been solved.

We had to make this into an election issue, so we hit the politicians where they paid the most attention. We commissioned a poll from one of the top polling firms in the country.

We asked for a reading of the population's thoughts on registration, assault weapons, and – Concordia paid for this one – a handgun ban.

The results were sweet.

When asked about registering all guns, 86 percent of the respondents were in favour, including 68 percent of gun-owning households. On the issue of banning assault weapons, 84 percent were in favour, including 71 percent of gun-owning households. And when it came to banning handguns, 71 percent were in favour, including 54 percent of gun-owning households.

The poll proved to be one of the best investments we ever made. It showed that people who supported more controls were a majority in every province, and in both rural and urban areas. We used the results as a news item, a tag ending for our releases and a quote for all occasions ("If the gun lobby truly represented most gun owners, they would *support* gun control.")

Unfortunately, the results by themselves did not affect the electoral debates. But they were just what we needed to kick off *our* election campaign.

❧

Our next step was to publicize the position of each party: what its policy was, how it had acted in the past, and what it intended to do about our demands. For the benefit of the media, we also compiled province-by-province accounts of where each candidate stood on the issue of further gun control. (This is why it had been important to get a registered vote on the last bill. Regardless of their current promises, we knew exactly where returning MPs had stood when they had had to pick sides.)

To remain absolutely impartial, we didn't endorse any party: our "candidates who made a difference" wore all political stripes, and so did the foes in our Hall of Shame.

Meanwhile, political allies were working behind the scenes to have the Liberal opposition support our objectives. After a long internal struggle, they managed to get the issue included among the promises in the party's Red Book – though not the elaborate vision that we had hoped for. Like all of the parties' election platforms, it shied away from controversial issues, and the only gun-control measures that were retained were those that no one argued with – such as harsher sentences for gun-related crimes.

Nonetheless, the presence of gun control in the Red Book was a significant achievement: it meant that the Liberal Party had committed itself to "act" on the issue.

Yet this *still* didn't rouse the media's interest in gun control.

Another press conference was called for. For novelty's sake, we decided to hold it in Quebec City, a place we had never been to before, and when the media showed up, we pulled out all the stops to prove that an increase in gun control was both popular and essential.

The reporters were puzzled. "Since you have so much support," one of them asked, "why are you getting so little response from the party leaders?"

How does one answer a question like that – were we supposed to concede that we lacked clout? I was still trying to
come up with an adequate retort when Hugh Brodie, the
assistant rector of Concordia, jumped into the fray.

"I believe *you* are the answer to that one," he said. "We're
doing everything we can to raise the issue, but in the end,
you're the ones who have access to the politicians. Shouldn't
you be asking them this very question?"

Journalists are usually not put on the spot like that, but
they accepted the challenge. As of that afternoon, the various
party leaders were questioned about our demands – and, for
a brief, shining moment, the subject was even broached
during the national televised debate.

It didn't land us an irreversible, binding commitment, but
the Liberal, NDP, and Bloc leaders all conceded that more
controls on guns were needed.

The Tories claimed the new gun law as a feather in its cap
– but said that the law needed no further strengthening. The
Reform Party, as expected, said tougher penalties was all that
was needed.

As the campaigns went on, cries of corruption, patronage
and kickbacks kept monopolizing the headlines, and by election night, a change in government had become a foregone
conclusion.

Like most Canadians, I sat glued to the TV throughout the
election results, watching the almighty Conservatives wither
away. Since most of them had been only reluctant supporters
of controls – and modest ones at that – I felt a little vindica-
tion as, riding by riding, seat by seat, they lost their power

and their privileges. Soon enough, all that remained was a party with four MPs. Then three. Then two . . .

Two: that's how many Tory MPs were still standing at the end of the count. The Liberals picked up most of the losses, and we ended up with a whole new government to contend with.

18

"Children are going to cease to participate in [shooting sports] because it is going to get too regulatory. . . . Children are going to say, 'I'm going to play golf. I'm going to play football.' Is that what the government wants?"

– George Duffy, Responsible Firearms Owners of Alberta

T hings are always slow after an election, especially when the reins of power change hands.

Between October 1993 and February 1994, the new MPS moved into their Ottawa offices, got acquainted with the permanent staff, and familiarized themselves with the most pressing issues. Having pressure groups to add more to the load was the furthest thing from their minds.

The new justice minister was Allan Rock, and the earliest we could reserve some time in his appointment book was on March 18. Which wasn't so bad considering that, over the first three years of our efforts, we had never even set foot in Kim Campbell's chambers.

The office we were invited to was much more impressive than the MPS' cramped quarters. Pierre Trudeau and Jean Chrétien had occupied the same rooms when they were justice ministers, and the entire place exuded History. The rooms were large, the windows high, the artwork impressive, and the furniture plush. We brought half a dozen people with us, and we still didn't fill all the sofas and comfy chairs. The classiest touch, however, was the coffee and cookies we were offered, which helped everyone feel more at home. Yet cookies were all we got out of the meeting.

We had kept our presentation simple and to the point, knowing that the more time spent on a song and dance, the less merit our case would seem to have. We presented our position as a moderate one, we showed how expensive guns were to health care, and when we got to the issue of registration, we pointed out that it didn't need to be introduced all at once. The measure, we said, could be gradually implemented, starting with new acquisitions from gun stores, and moving on to all guns over an extended period.

The minister listened politely to everything we said, but before he could respond, one of the department officials piped up:

"Your proposals are very interesting. But I hear that their efficiency is still being questioned."

"Actually," countered Wendy, "the experts aren't divided at all." She started to run through the organizations that endorsed our position, but he cut her short.

"I know about your supporters, thank you. But we can't rush into this. We'll need a lot more proof that registration will work."

Bolts of lightning shot out of Wendy's eyes. From the very beginning of our campaign, this official had tried to undermine our arguments regarding registration. In spite of the superficially pleasant atmosphere, the tension between the two had reached saturation point.

She cocked her head and smiled sweetly.

"More proof. Yes, well – *listen here*. You've been sitting through a detailed presentation by the most knowledgeable specialists in the country. We handed you the best studies available on the matter. They all support our claims, and they have done so for years, unchallenged by any credible expert. Of course, anyone would like to be absolutely certain every time a new rule is envisioned, but most laws, including our earlier gun-control laws, have actually been adopted with much *less* proof than we've brought in. So my question is, *exactly how much more do you want, and why should registration be held to this exceptional standard?*"

"Hear, hear," said the president of the Canadian Association of Chiefs of Police, and we almost broke into spontaneous applause.

Allan Rock allowed himself a diplomatic chuckle.

"Point well taken," he said briskly, sparing his underling the trouble of wiggling his way out of this one.

The conversation was drawing to a close, so I made one last point before anyone got up to leave.

"You know," I said, "no matter what you decide, no matter how strong or weak a legislation is, the gun lobby will fight it tooth and nail, just like it did when the previous bill was introduced. Why only go halfway, then? I say, if you're going to do it, do it right."

He gave me another smile. "I'll keep that in mind," he said. He tapped the files that sat on the table next to him. "We'll take a good look at all this, and I'd like to congratulate you for doing such a thorough job. Still, in the time I have spent here, I've come to understand what a complex issue this is, and I'm sure you'll agree that we do have to listen to all sides. We'll get back to you as soon as we can."

"That went over well," I said as we stepped into the elevator.

Wendy, however, was uncharacteristically quiet, and after our supporters left she broke into deep wracking sobs.

*

"Nothing," she kept repeating. "They're not going to do anything. Not now, not ever."

I tried to reassure her, but her distress was rather frightening. Wasn't this the woman who had confronted roomfuls of angry gun owners? Until now, no meeting had ever had such an effect on her, and for the life of me, I couldn't see what had gone wrong.

"Surely you hadn't expected a commitment on our first encounter?"

"Yes, I did! We've waited so long and worked so hard for this. He should have given us more than this 'We'll think about it' bullshit!"

"Give him a chance. It's not like he rejected our demands."

"Didn't you hear that department guy ramble on about needing more proof? I just had to blast him, even though I knew I shouldn't . . ."

"What are you talking about? He was asking for it, and you really put him in his place!"

"That's the problem, I came down too hard. It wasn't very professional."

"If that's what's troubling you, don't even worry about it. The minister himself seemed amused."

"Oh, *come on*. He said, 'It's a complex issue'! He's going to be a politician about this!"

"Wendy, there were too many people there for him to commit to anything. Look, he listened and we made a great impression. For now, that's all we can ask."

"Still feels like we're back at square one to me."

We squirmed and wondered and fretted, but our anxiety didn't last long. After four weeks, during which he met with a few other groups, Rock announced to the media that "tougher gun control" would be introduced during the coming year.

Our relief was tremendous when we heard the news, but we stopped short of jumping for joy. The announcement hadn't mentioned any specifics. This could still mean as little as an increase in the penalties for gun crimes – not exactly what we defined as improved controls.

In response to the news, we issued a positive statement: "It's about time someone had the courage to stand up to the gun lobby." But we were firm on one point – we wouldn't settle for another watered-down bill: "We need a strong national response."

The future looked pretty good. I was beginning to hope.

Then all hell broke loose.

19

"It's not over, not by a long shot. Now we're going to get mean."

– Ed Begin, executive director,
Saskatchewan Wildlife Federation

Ever since the election, the gun lobby had been uncannily quiet. And with good reason: as long as the government hadn't announced that it would act on gun control, they couldn't rouse gun owners into action. They only flexed their muscles when they perceived an actual threat.

And what muscles they were! When Allan Rock embarked on cross-country consultations, crowds of gun enthusiasts greeted him at every stop. They overran every town-hall meeting, where all attempts to discuss the issue in a rational manner rapidly gave way to angry diatribes, with little room for dissent ("Adolf Hitler supported gun control"). An impartial observer could have been excused for believing that the country was 95 percent against restrictions on guns.

"I'm here to see if any common ground can be found," Rock said repeatedly. "You claim that registration is too complex, costly, and burdensome, but *if* it was simple, inexpensive, and unobtrusive, how would you feel about it?"

No dice. Some rallies didn't even wait for the formal consultation: they sent the message to any local MP that leaning in favour of gun control was politically dangerous. The demonstrations in one area affected the climate in the next. When MPs saw what was happening next door, they took it as a warning: the same furor could just as easily materialize in their riding.

There wasn't much we could do about any of it. We'd hear about most rallies at the last minute, then scramble like crazy to get a few sympathizers to show up.

It was a thankless job. Our supporters would be outnumbered by anywhere from fifty to a thousand opponents. The fear of being harassed dissuaded all but the most dedicated. The presence of the media at these events wasn't much of a mitigating factor. At one demonstration in New Brunswick, a supporter of ours, wearing a sandwich board in praise of gun control, managed to slip in between the cameras and the protesters. He was immediately knocked to the ground and assaulted, right in front of the reporters!

Then why did we ask our friends to go? To start with, Wendy and I couldn't possibly attend each event ourselves. More to the point, it would have made us look like the only people in the country demanding tighter controls. If other men and women made themselves heard, they would show the other side of the conflict. And so they would be included in the media's coverage of these events.

This was Plan A, and it would happen only *if* they made

themselves heard. More often than not, we had to resort to Plan B, which was to get a couple of quotes from local authorities, put them in a press release with the contacts' phone numbers, and fax them to news outlets a day before the scheduled meeting. And then we'd move on to the next protest.

That, in a nutshell, was our summer – one rally after another, every week or so. We were always in defensive mode, and we were getting clobbered. It felt like fixing leaks on a sinking ship, and we came closer to despair with every setback.

It must have been hard for the minister, as well – anyone in his situation would have developed doubts about his pro-control views. Even the civil servants in his department, who had been mildly helpful when we got the previous bill passed, now advised him against further changes, which they considered either unnecessary or beyond reach.

We knew that some people would say that this was democracy at work. If no one stood up for gun control, how could we claim that the majority of people were on our side?

These were valid questions. But they didn't take into account several factors:

• A loud minority is still a minority. Protesters may express themselves in a boisterous way but it doesn't follow that they speak for everyone.

• Mobs can be misinformed. Organizers often make exaggerated claims, and their recruits end up protesting against fictional problems.

• There is such a thing as fake grassroots. Bussed-in agitators can always make up for a low turnout.

• Demonstrations aren't the sole yardstick. A solid study counts for more than a waving fist.

• Complaining is easy. Finding solutions is much harder and calls for more effort.

Regrettably, none of this counts for anything in the public eye. There was no way around it. We knew that, sooner or later, we would have to strike big in order to compensate for the disastrous summer.

Ironically, it was the gun lobby itself that provided us with the perfect opportunity. In a widely circulated notice, it announced that they would end their campaign of protests with one last rally in the most strategic of locations.

GUN OWNERS ARE FED UP

Gun owners from across the country plan to march on Parliament Hill this September. The rally is being organized by Firearms Enthusiasts Demanding Unbiased Policy (FED UP), the name taken on by the Sportsmen's Alliance created earlier this year in Ontario to foster communications between gun clubs and firearm organizations. . . .

"Our objective is to emphasize to the federal politicians that firearm owners and users are no longer complacent," said [co-ordinator Don] Sellers. We are tired of being the scapegoat of the whole political problem."

As part of its fight against crime, the federal government has said it will consider further gun-control regulations this fall, including a possible handgun ban and a national gun registry. The alliance believes the crime problem lies not with gun control, but with the faulty enforcement of laws, gun smuggling, and lenient immigration policies.

To make these concerns known, the alliance has asked Prime Minister Jean Chrétien and Justice Minister Allan Rock to address the crowd during a mass rally on Parliament Hill that starts at noon, Thursday, September 22.

"We want as many people as possible," said Sellers. "This is going to be a controlled but visible demonstration."

Of all the demonstrations there had been across the country, this was the one we *had* to sink.

ॐ

The idea of droves of gun owners converging on Parliament Hill had initially been very unsettling, but before long, we started thinking about it in more positive terms.

For the previous four years, we had constantly tried to warn the public that the gun lobby wielded enough political influence to hijack the public agenda (Wendy's words). But most Canadians weren't aware that rallies in small- and medium-sized towns had any such effect. Whenever an MP openly started defending pro-gun interests, it rarely rated any space in the newspapers. It was easy for people to think of the rallies as isolated incidents, happening far, far away. They would see no need to panic, thinking that support for gun control was still strong everywhere else.

A demonstration in the capital was very different, though. This was, after all, the decision-making centre of the nation.

All of a sudden, the gun lobby's strength would be on prominent display.

What better time was there to exploit their weaknesses?
Like martial arts practitioners do, we could make the size of
our opponents work in our favour, and reap the benefits of
their pressure tactics. If we played our cards right, couldn't
we turn their rally into a backdrop for *our* message?

To make that happen, we devised a three-punch strategy:

One: In anticipation of the protesters' arguments, we drew
up a package that grouped all of our arguments in ten tightly
packed categories. But unlike our usual press releases, this
one was not short and sweet. We attached the actual studies,
with all the crucial passages marked and identified.

It was an unconventional move for any lobby group, whose
coverage usually consists of a brief sound bite on TV news-
casts, but we felt we could risk it. Our information packages
had an excellent reputation among journalists, and since we
started off with a concise summary, the size of the appendixes
was of little consequence. We were saying, "Don't take our
word for it – see for yourselves."

Both inside the Centre Block of Parliament and across the
street, there are press galleries where all the news correspon-
dents have their own mailboxes. Three days before the
demonstration, we delivered three hundred kits to each mail
room. We also sent a kit to any journalist, columnist, or editorialist who had ever covered gun control, as well as to all
members of Parliament.

On several occasions in the past, we had managed to
publish our texts as op-ed pieces, but this particular mailing

got our arguments into the editorials, many of which directly quoted from our documents. Given how much attention politicians grant these pages, we knew the impact would be considerable.

Two: The day before the demonstration, we assembled our best panel of experts yet for a press conference inside the Parliament.

Firearm enthusiasts, they said, all too often cast themselves as experts in the matter of gun-related crime prevention. While they *were* adept at cleaning, loading, and using their weapons, this did not make them authorities on public safety – no more than cigarettes turned smokers into health-care professionals. To evaluate the effectiveness of the controls, one had to look elsewhere.

The conference was aimed at the reporters who would be filing early stories to announce the upcoming demonstration. We wanted these reports (GUN LOBBY TO HOLD HUGE RALLY ON PARLIAMENT HILL) to be balanced right away (COALITION OF MAJOR PLAYERS SHOWS PUBLIC SUPPORT FOR GUN CONTROL).

Three: Despite these precautions, we knew we still needed to prevent our opponents from having the last word. But since a counter-demonstration was out of the question, we turned the floor over to the most forgotten people in the debate . . . the victims.

However inconvenient gun owners felt the new law would be – the red tape, the permit fees, the government intrusion – no comparison was possible with all the deaths and injuries that the measures would prevent.

To put the gun lobby's objections in perspective, they would only need to tell their stories.

As simple as it seems, it's a lot to ask of people whose lives have just been turned upside down. They had nothing to gain personally from such a painful experience – most of them were still mourning their own loss. If they chose to help, it would be because they *wanted* to, not because they were told they *should*.

Reluctantly, seven of them agreed to brave the cameras.

The rules of politics, media, and demonstrations were so alien to them, it was like juggling knives. This would be the main event, the one that would go head to head against a rally of ten thousand, and we had no control over the way it would go!

Two hours before the rally, Wendy and I watched the press conference from my MP's office on the Parliament's closed-circuit channel (the group was using the Centre Block's press room). They all looked nervous, but they seemed to be holding up. That wasn't enough to reassure us, however. There was still a wild card left.

One victim's parent, Kim Forbes, had shown up only a half hour earlier. Unlike the others, she hadn't been briefed. She didn't know what to say, and she was very shaken up: it hadn't been long since the death of her son, and the case against the owner of the gun that had been used was still before the courts.

Since she hadn't prepared a statement, the group arranged for her to go last, trusting that the other testimonies would guide her own. But that also meant she would be leaving the final impression. . . .

Robert McNamara, the spokesperson for Victims of Violence, stood up and welcomed everyone. He described why the seven of them had come together as a group, and why they had decided to speak out:

"The demonstrators who are gathering outside argue that gun control will interfere with their hobbies. But what's really at stake is the right of the whole population to be protected. There may seem to be a lot of protesters on the Hill later on, but thousands are also shot every year, and for every one of these victims, there are families whose lives are irreparably damaged.

"Some of these people are here today."

He was the first to tell his story. His brother, he explained, was killed after being dragged into an argument. The man he was fighting with left, came back with a handgun, and shot him in cold blood.

Suzanne Laplante-Edward, who was the next up, spoke of the fourteen young women who had been gunned down on December 6. She made the point that the killer had used a legally acquired assault weapon.

She passed the microphone to Anne-Marie Fletcher, who said her brother had been one of three people killed during a robbery in a McDonald's in Nova Scotia. The murderer had stolen the handgun he used from his girlfriend's stepfather.

The next speaker was a survivor. A police officer, Walter Filipas had been shot twice in the head when he stopped a man armed with a stolen pistol. When his partner tried to assist him, she had also been shot in the face and thigh.

Mark Hogben then spoke of how his father had died, along with three other professors at Concordia University. Fabrikant had belonged to a gun club, and had used a semi-automatic pistol that he had legally purchased, as well as two other revolvers that he had obtained through his wife.

Next to Mark was Jim Leimonis Dimitrios, the father of a teenage girl who was shot and killed in Toronto during yet another restaurant robbery. The murderer had used a sawed-off shotgun, which had not been recovered.

And then came Kim's turn.

She had grown very pale – the cameras and microphones obviously intimidated her. With trembling fingers, she held up a picture of her son, saying, "This is Matthew," and burst into tears. She covered her eyes, tried to control herself, but it was just too much. Someone in the audience said, "Take your time, ma'am," and we all waited for a minute or so, until she caught her breath.

"I'm sorry," she whispered. "I can't get used to this."

She explained about the house she had visited with her child to purchase a used bike a few months earlier. Neighbourhood teenagers were hanging around on the main floor, where there were a dozen guns linked by a chain that they quickly broke open. The next thing Kim knew, she was staring at her son in a morgue, a tag on his toe and his insides blown apart.

She described how the bullet had torn through him, and all the damage it had done. "A blast of a shotgun to an eight-year-old little boy's body is so devastating," she sobbed. "It's killing me day by day by day."

It couldn't have been more gut-wrenching. We were crying with her, the other parents cried with her, even the reporters cried with her.

It was her picture and testimony that made the papers, right beside the demonstrators brandishing FED UP placards. They were both powerful images. The question was, who would people feel more sympathy for?

We already knew the answer.

20

"They're two women — that's it. Just two women who believe in a utopian world."

— Lawrence Belec, Canadian Firearms Action Council

The ten thousand protesters who came to the rally were a great help to our cause. According to the accounts of media commentators, they came off as rude, selfish, rowdy and, as a group, very very scary. Best of all, they made Allan Rock look like a hero.

"We're not out to take away your hunting rifles," he said from the podium, his voice barely audible above the boos and the catcalls. "But one thing should be clear. We *are* going to have a gun-control package this fall, and it's going to include controls on long guns."

It still wasn't a commitment to registration. But the fact that he dared to refer to more controls on rifles and shotguns in front of an angry mob hinted that the bill might not be a disappointment after all. . . .

Of course, the media didn't all side with us, and we got our share of criticism. "The pro-control lobby bordered on indecency when it displayed the sorrow of mourning families for all to see," commented one editorialist. Another questioned, "Why this is a priority now, in the face of a monstrous debt and an antiquated social system?"

I could take these arguments from a stranger – but not a friend. A few weeks later, I was chatting with a group of Poly graduates in a trendy bar on Saint-Denis when one of them made a similar remark upon hearing of my recent activities: "You know, Heidi, if you really want to eliminate violence, you're going after the wrong target . . ."

I forced a smile. In five years, I had learned to recognize certain arguments from the outset, and when people talked of "eliminating" violence, it usually meant they wouldn't support a measure that was just a part of the solution.

"Oh really?"

"Yes. Guns are secondary. You should be fighting poverty. If everybody worked, no one would harbour any resentment and there would be no more violence."

Oh, la-di-dah, Mister Philosopher, did you figure that out by yourself? I'm sooo impressed.

I had never before exploded in someone's face, but he paid for all the others. After having spent the last few months constantly refuting gun-lobby rhetoric, I had no patience left for idealistic debates.

"All right then, tell you what we'll do. Found your own movement, bring poverty to an end, and in five years we'll compare results. In the meantime, do you *mind* if I try to reduce gun-related deaths, or do you think I should do more while you go back to your lucrative job on Monday morning?

Go on, I just love it when people who are wrapped up in their career advise me on what *other* cause I should be working on!"

Everyone at the table was taken aback, and I instantly regretted my sarcasm. I vowed to keep my temper in check the next time around, but for a minute there, the release was terribly gratifying.

⁂

Rock's announcement at the September rally that the bill would be ready that fall meant that the cabinet must have approved his plans. And announcing the deadline so publicly left him no choice but to follow through. Since the Liberals came to power, one December 6 had already gone by without any news; if he was still empty-handed on the fifth anniversary of the massacre, his credibility would be badly damaged.

He didn't make it. He never could have. No matter how many people he assigned to the project, a complex national policy cannot be drawn up in so short a time.

Instead, he did the next best thing. On December 1, the Justice Department invited us back to Ottawa for the "unveiling of the proposals." Not the actual bill, but a detailed outline of all the measures that *would* be in it. Revealing them would prove that progress was being made, and it would give everyone something to celebrate on the anniversary itself.

All they told us was "Come on down, we think you'll like this." But the subtext was unmistakable: *Get your partners on standby*. Pro-gun representatives would also be there – albeit in a different room – and our public reactions would have to overshadow theirs.

Our hearts were racing! We knew we shouldn't rejoice yet, but it was hard not to let it go straight to our heads. We thought, *This is it! This could be everything we've been fighting for!*

Flashback to the spring of 1992. Bill C-17 has passed a few months ago, and I'm taking advantage of a rare lull in my schedule to help my parents with their landscaping chores in preparation for the summer. The skies are clear, the apple trees are in bloom, and there's just enough of a breeze to take the edge off the heat. I'm raking the needles from under the pine trees – don't know why, it'll just mean more grass to mow – when my mother joins me, watering can in hand.

Her attitude has changed a lot since my departure from Bell, and she now shares my enthusiasm for the cause (she handed out our postcards to everyone she knew, and even pushed them on strangers in the shopping centre). Still, there's a slight hesitation in her voice when she asks me how long I'll keep working for the coalition. Wouldn't this be a good time to go back to engineering?

I think about it for a moment. It's true that I sometimes feel tired: our revenues are down, Wendy and I are struggling to keep people interested, and I don't want to chase rainbows for the rest of my life. That's sort of how I see universal registration: an impossible dream.

I look up at her.

"But Mom," I say, "wouldn't it be the most amazing accomplishment to get all that we're asking for? Look at what is going on in the States: as long as we've got a chance to avoid the same fate, don't you think it's worth a try? *Imagine if we succeed!"*

❧

Now, the moment of truth was upon us.

Wendy and I spent the following week sending urgent notes to all of our supporters, asking them to prepare positive press releases to be sent out the moment the announcement of Rock's proposals was made. As soon as we found out more, we'd have a volunteer forward the proposals to them, along with our comments.

The plan was to ensure that within hours of the unveiling, every newsroom in the country would have usable quotes in support of the proposals coming out of its fax machines.

On the eve of the announcement, we checked into our usual hotel. But anticipation, fear, and excitement were all mingled in our minds, and we ended up talking halfway through the night.

"This is it, Wendy, this is it! The end is finally in sight!"

"Hey, slow down. You know very well that we could get a bad surprise."

"Oh, relax. They're quite aware of what we want. If they sound so confident, it must be because they know we'll be applauding the proposals!"

"Well, they did seem to expect furious reactions from the other side. That's always a good sign!"

"Just think: yesterday, we couldn't even get them to say the word *registration*! Do you realize how much progress we've made in five years?"

"Go to sleep, Heidi. We have a long day ahead of us and we need our rest."

"Are you serious? This is a historical moment: WE BEAT THE GUN LOBBY! Are you *really* feeling sleepy?"

"No, but if you don't stop bouncing around like that, I'm warning you, I'm going to ask for another room!"

We were so thrilled it seemed as if we'd never come down. But as soon as we settled into our seats in the Justice Department's conference room along with our allies, we became focussed and alert. We took frantic notes throughout the department's slide projection, and when we got to the print-outs that completed the presentation, we were surprised to find that each of our demands could be checked off. Everything we wanted was there, including registration. The package even included a partial handgun ban, in response to Concordia University's campaign.

In our minds, we were already composing the press release that we would issue an hour later: "The prime minister promised the strongest possible gun control, and it looks as if the justice minister intends to deliver."

We reminded ourselves to remain vigilant with respect to hidden flaws. We kept grilling the department officials, "Will *all* guns be registered?" "Will there be exceptions for existing assault weapons?" We knew from experience that loopholes could ruin the best of intentions, and we were well aware that the gun enthusiasts in the next room would exploit them to their fullest.

"Draft legislation is draft legislation. We have a long way to go before this becomes law."

Still, if the bill matched these proposals, we wouldn't have much to complain about.

"We are saying to the minister, 'Don't back down.' We only hope that he is able to stand his ground."

21

"I have a small shotgun and, somewhere in this world, I have a .22. I have no idea where it is."

— Bob Mitchell, Saskatchewan justice minister

Bill C-68 was tabled in the House of Commons on Valentine's Day, 1995.

Fourteen victims — February fourteenth. In the world of PR, these things are rarely a coincidence.

The important thing was that, except for a single concession to the gun lobby, the legislation respected the proposals in every way. (The one concession was that current owners of newly banned guns were allowed to keep these weapons and trade them among themselves. Since their ranks would decrease in time, we found it an acceptable compromise.)

Were we happy? Absolutely. For the first time ever, the government was on our side. By mid-April, the bill passed both first and second readings and was ready to be reviewed by another parliamentary committee. As long as everything went well there. . . .

But we knew from experience that the next downturn in our fortunes couldn't be too far ahead.

＊

Wendy was terribly disappointed, and she made no secret of it.

"What do you mean, there's no story? You attended our presentation during the previous hearings, and that bill wasn't half as important as this one!"

The reporter groaned in mock exasperation. "That's exactly it," he explained. "Last time, you were *critical* of the bill. That was something we could report on."

"But if you dismiss current support as boring, then dissent is all you will report, and that will slant the entire coverage!"

Wendy spoke from experience. Just that week, the Canadian Bar Association had testified in favour the bill, but since they had expressed concerns about the wording pertaining to search and seizure procedures, the headline had come out PROPOSED LAW UNCONSTITUTIONAL, LAW GROUP SAYS. And when the Canadian Medical Association stated that the effectiveness of registration was an unanswered question, the papers twisted this into MDS REJECT REGISTRATION IN GUN BILL.

"So what do you want us to do, say 'Gun-Control Group Supports Gun-Control Bill'? Big news!"

"Oh, right – there can't possibly be news if there is no conflict. I suppose you'd be more interested in the bricks I'm getting in the mail than a bill that will save lives."

"Wait a minute. What's this about bricks?"

"The latest idea of the New Brunswick Firearms Alliance. They're trying to deplete our finances by sending me bricks, manure, and soiled underpants, c.o.d. You don't want to know."

Pause.

"Have you kept the bricks? We could send a photographer . . ."

We hadn't really thought about it. The crank calls and the libel attempts weren't exactly rare – a so-called "freelance" reporter would even go so far as to visit Wendy's high school in order to dig up damning information on her past. After a while, we didn't pay any attention to such tactics.

Which didn't mean that we took them lightly. Ever since the guy with the hunting knife showed up, I had learned to live with these incidents, whether they were real or imagined. There was no stress, no fear: the habits I developed quickly became mere reflexes, like my making sure I have my keys on me when I leave my apartment.

I never saw anyone without an appointment. I only gave my address to reputable charities. My telephone number was unlisted. My office door was not identified. And if I ever thought I was followed – a hostile glance or a prolonged stare was all it took – I'd step out of the subway train at the very last second, rollerblade against traffic on a one-way street, or add a few stores onto my itinerary until I was sure I had lost my "pursuer."

Apparently, this type of anecdote held more appeal for the media than our testimony in favour of the bill. Thanks to the bricks, we did get a good article out of it, along with a lasting lesson about newsworthiness.

From here on, it wouldn't be our support for the bill that made headlines, but our clashes with our opponents.

❦

"They want conflict? We'll give them conflict."

Regardless of the media's appetite for drama, we hadn't planned to sit on the sidelines during the hearings on Bill C-68 anyway. The last time around, we had been too busy dealing with the whip to do much else, but for this bill, we intended to make the most of every step.

Long before the committee received the legislation, we had asked all of our allies to put in a request to be heard, and we helped them prepare their briefs. During the next weeks, we wrote reams of analyses – eight hundred pages in all – about the bill's every feature, and we passed the information on to whomever we thought could use it.

Now our focus would shift.

Defending your views is all well and good, but discrediting the opposition can be just as effective. Throughout the hearings, we organized one media event after another to match our opponents' testimonies, exposing their weaknesses for all to see.

And every night, we faxed sample questions and related documents to the committee members who seemed to support the bill. If they felt like putting these queries to the pro-gun witnesses scheduled for the next day, it was entirely up to them:

• To Taylor Buckner, from the *Regroupement pour une gestion efficace des armes à feu*: According to what you said in a televised interview, the only reason that you see behind the bill is linked to the separation of Quebec. Can you explain this to us?

• To Judith Ross, target shooter: In a recent article, you were quoted as saying that "the police are hiding behind the skirts of the Coalition in order to further their own agenda, which is to be the only ones with guns." What evidence do you have to support this claim?

• To the Responsible Firearms Owners of Manitoba: A brochure from your organization says "The Justice Minister intends to ban all guns." Might this be the reason many gun owners attended your rally?

• To the Responsible Firearms Owners of Alberta: You've worked on an advertising campaign which says, "Every day, more law-abiding citizens are making a conscious decision not to register their firearms." Do you feel that this is how a "law-abiding citizen" behaves?

• To any one of the provincial Responsible Firearms Owners: Given that 60 percent of gun homicides are committed by first-time offenders, isn't it likely that, in most cases, "responsible" gun owners misuse their firearms?

• To Bryan Hodges, president of the International Practical Shooting Confederation of Canada: On your club's shooting course, what does the target look like?

That last question may seem innocuous, but it created quite a stir.

"It's a steel plate that's about twenty-five inches high, and that falls down when it's hit," Hodges replied.

"It's a target that I think has a human shape . . ." insisted the MP, Pierrette Venne.

"First, I didn't design the target; it's been around for about fifteen years. Second, for an average six-foot person, the target stands about the height of your belt."

The MP, who was about 5'4", checked the information we had sent in.

"This target is forty-two inches high, and not twenty-five," she remarked.

Another committee member, Paddy Torsney, rose to her feet and pulled out a plate that had been given her.

"I'd suggest to you that this –" she adjusted the silhouette in front of her body "– is about the size of my upper torso," she said. "Anything that's a hot target for both the face area and the heart area would in fact suggest that you teach people to shoot at other civilians. Do you think people should be arming themselves and practising defensive shooting like this?"

The man tried to dig himself out by stating that the design of the plate was recognized internationally and that he was surprised anyone would delve into such areas – but he had already lost the battle. No matter how long he spoke about "constructive ways to go about amending this legislation," as he put it, he could not erase the impression that the silhouette had left.

Alas, all our efforts had little discernable effect on the outcome of the hearings. We had hoped that the bill would come out stronger, but instead, we only prevented things from getting worse.

A case in point was the attempt to decriminalize first offences related to registration.

The bill said that all firearms would have to be registered, even the old Winchester that Grampa left in the attic before he passed away. If his widow failed to report it, should she be subjected to the full penalties of the law?

"Let's not go overboard," pro-gun politicians said. "This should be like parking tickets: everyone should get some kind of warning, along with the benefit of the doubt for their first offence. An honest mistake shouldn't brand these citizens with a criminal record!"

This only makes sense when applied to Grandma, and when one forgets that police officers *can* choose not to lay charges when it's an honest mistake. (This had been the case with handguns for years, so why would it have been any different for rifles and shotguns?) But what about biker gangs who bury their arsenal in the backyard, as well as the multitude of gun owners who threatened to do just that if the law was passed? Should these people be able to claim forgetfulness and get off with a mere "parking ticket"?

This kind of argument made my blood boil. Without proper incentive, gun owners would be able to disregard the law until they got caught once, and only then would they feel compelled to abide by the rules.

Dangerous as it was, the amendment to decriminalize first offences could very well squeeze through: the six opposition

MPs (Reform and Bloc) were in favour, and two of the eight Liberals had hinted that they liked the amendment. If only one more of the minister's colleagues supported the amendment, the vote would be tied. Two, and the amendment was in.

Seeing the Bloc align itself with the Reformers gave us quite a jolt. After all, both university massacres had occurred in Quebec!

Not wanting to antagonize longtime allies when there was still a chance they'd change their minds, we trod as lightly as we could . . . but our indignation over their betrayal was still apparent in our communiqués.

The press immediately picked up on it, writing virulent editorials and publishing readers' letters that expressed their dismay in no uncertain terms. *Decriminalizing first-time offenses would give a green light to anybody intent on disobeying the law*, shouted an editorial in *Le Devoir*. *Has the opposition gone completely mad?* added a reader in the *Globe and Mail*.

We tried everything we could to put the party back on track. I talked to one aide after another, discussed the issue with any Bloc MP who would listen, and even managed to meet their leader, Lucien Bouchard, for a heart-to-heart.

Apparently, he had never heard of the police's concerns. A representative of the Canadian Chiefs of Police had accompanied me, and when he laid them out for him, Bouchard was quite surprised.

One MP's assistant told me that we *had* convinced him, but since they expected all eight members of the Liberal Party to block the amendment, they felt it made their opinions irrelevant. "They figured they may as well appease the gun lobby in the rural ridings," is how he put it to me. "You know, so we can tell them 'See? We tried to weaken the bill. . . .' "

I was aghast. Even if the gun lobby was fooled by this empty gesture, what had happened to the Bloc's earlier displays of principles, as well as their respect for the wishes of the vast majority of their constituents?

As it turned out, their decision to support the amendments *was* inconsequential – though not for the reason they had expected.

Rock had already decided to search for a compromise that would satisfy all the major players. We all put our heads together, and came up with the following terms:

If someone *knowingly* refused to register a gun, then this first offence would be a criminal act. The failure to get an owner's licence would always be criminal. And, no matter what the impediments, a final deadline for the implementation (January 1, 2003) would be enshrined in the law.

The third part alone was worth the concessions. The way the bill had originally been written, the enforcement dates of the transition period would have been postponed by subsequent regulations, and could easily have been pushed back every time a snag was encountered. If this occurred often enough, the law would be meaningless.

When the minister testified at the hearings the next day, he all but dictated what he was willing to accept and what recommendations should be forwarded to the House. His message was clear. If his Liberal colleagues valued their standing in the party, no other part of the bill was to be touched.

The other changes the committee recommended to the House of Commons were minor, and Bill C-68 was adopted by a strong majority a few days later.

All that we now needed was the Senate's approval, and since it had called for these very measures when it passed the previous bill, there was no reason to worry, was there?

Ha!

22

"What kind of a society are we promoting, when the infantilized citizen has to lock up the gun he keeps at home? A free man doesn't treat his own children this way."

— Pierre Lemieux, author, *Le Droit de porter des armes*

Put yourself in his shoes.

He's the head of the party that lost most of its seats during the last elections. He used to rub elbows with the elite, commanding respect and deference, and now his party doesn't even have official status in the Parliament. He's got to start over, find new backers, embark on a membership drive.

But what can he use as a power base? Why, the Senate, of course.

Unlike MPs, senators are appointed, not elected, and are usually loyal to the party whose leader gave them their job. There are 104 seats in the Senate. Four of them were vacant, three held by independents, and 46 aligned with the Liberal Party. The majority, 51, belonged to the Progressive Conservative Party.

It hardly mattered that Jean Charest had been elected in the heart of the province that was 90 percent in favour of gun control. His concerns as Conservative leader lay less with representing his constituents than with rebuilding his party. As a one-issue group with its back to the wall, the gun community was a perfect target for recruitment: if he implied that he controlled half the Senate, he might just be able to attract new members among those who wanted the bill stopped – quickly and in sufficient numbers.

"The gun registry won't work," he said on a western tour. "I would back off and focus on stronger penalties," and "They should invest in other things."

With a great sigh, Wendy flew back out west to buttress our network. As for me, I got saddled with the job of discrediting Charest and exposing his agenda.

A tall order – in more than one respect.

The teachers, the whip, and the gun lobbyists – those I could deal with. Though I loathe confrontation, I'm perfectly capable of taking the bull by the horns to defend what I believe in. It's when logic and persuasion don't get me anywhere that I'm stumped. Raising my voice, wielding threats, or resorting to force, that's not part of my arsenal. And to attack someone for the sole purpose of making him squirm? Way off the scale for me.

I grew up in an extremely peaceful family. My parents never argued in front of me and my sisters, and I found myself completely defenceless when taunted in grade school (just try being a child of recent immigrants, with a name like mine, then we'll talk). The jeers left no long-lasting scars, but the underlying cruelty profoundly marked me: I vowed never to sink to that level, no matter how deserved the treatment was, or how much good could come out of it.

I didn't even know what kind of offensive I could mount against Charest. He had evaded us for years, and I couldn't see how I'd get him to sit still for ten seconds.

But I didn't have much choice. We had already shown him in what way the legislation would promote public safety. We had explained how his support would benefit his image. We had tried every argument under the heading of Reason and Common Sense. The only thing he seemed to respond to was how his opposition to the bill would further his career – never mind that lives were at stake.

Those who live by the sword . . . attract similar trouble. To make sure his position became a bad political choice, we needed to generate negative consequences, and it had to hurt.

I didn't want to think about it. All summer long, I gradually crossed off every item on my "to do" list except that one, as if the task were too unpleasant to warrant my attention. It was only on August 1 that the gravity of my inaction finally hit home. If I didn't strike hard and quick, the threat to the legislation would only build.

Suddenly frantic, I made a few appointments and caught a bus to his Sherbrooke riding, hoping that I could play it by ear.

I discovered when I got there that Charest had kept such a low profile on gun control that nobody knew his real position. I briefed the police, the health departments, the women's organizations, the local victims' group – everyone was stunned.

Just being there netted me four articles and one editorial, plus interviews in the electronic media. But the best part was when I let it slip that Charest wouldn't meet with me. One journalist checked, and his aide denied that it had been intentional. By the time I got back home, she had left an invitation on my answering machine to meet with him on August 17.

If he thought we would meet quietly, he was gravely mistaken. When I showed up, I brought all the local reporters with me. My shaking hands with him in front of his office door was a great photo opportunity, and if they waited to hear my impressions afterward, I could make it worth their while.

We usually never involve the media when meeting with a politician, but I was certain that talking to Charest would be like talking to a Teflon wall, and that this would be the only way to extract anything positive from the encounter.

I was right. First he put forward an erroneous assumption: "Through the Firearm Acquisition Certificate program, the federal government knows who owns legal weapons."

I explained what was wrong with the claim. "FACs are for *buying* guns, not owning them; not only do they expire after five years, but the whole system is so recent that two-thirds of all current owners don't have one."

He let this bounce off him, and proceeded to another worn-out argument: "Ninety percent of all firearms involved in crimes are illegally owned."

To put it succinctly, he never acknowledged that any of his assumptions were mistaken – not even when the police wrote to him to set the record straight.

After the meeting I pointed out the pro-gun slant of his

position to the media, which created a lot of interest. He tried to remain evasive but, prodded by one of the dailies, he was forced to reveal his game plan. His party, said the article in *La Presse*, "is strongly opposed to the gun-control bill and intends to use its majority in the Senate to amend it substantially."

This was of critical importance, since it was the first time he had gone on record about intervening at the state level. Picture it: a party with two elected seats out of 295, planning to obstruct the will of the entire House of Commons!

Soon after our meeting, I set up a big press conference in his riding, at which more than twenty local groups vigorously expressed their support for the bill.

Charest must have been startled by the uproar, because he promptly invited everyone who had taken part in the press conference to a meeting in a nearby community centre. I don't know if he expected the groups to keep the invitation to themselves, but they did just the opposite. Not only was I asked to attend, but just before the meeting took place, I spent an hour instructing them, like an army sergeant.

"This is what he'll say about the types of weapons used in crime . . . Here are the statistics that you, the police, can counter him with. This is what he'll say about murders committed with guns . . . Here are the facts about domestic violence that you, the women's groups, can use to back your own experience . . ."

I *had* to be ruthless. The man oozed enough charisma to mesmerize anyone – some of these people had even worked on his election campaign! But I got them all primed up and by the time he entered the room, he didn't stand a chance.

He shook hands with everyone. He then recited the *exact* arguments that he had used with me. He was very charming, very confident, very convincing. Had I not warned them beforehand, I wouldn't have been surprised if he had won them over.

I never opened my mouth. When Charest was done, each spokesperson took issue with one or another of his arguments. Some started with praise like, "We've always been big supporters of yours," or "We have your name on a plaque by the door of our women's shelter . . ." and followed up with ". . . now we're ashamed of it!" One after the other, they tore through his beautiful speech. Nobody backed down.

By the end of the meeting, his face was bright red and he made a beeline for the exit.

The groups stayed behind. Now that they had had a taste of their own strength, they asked what more they could do. I suggested they write an article that summarized their response to his position. They did and it was later published in three different papers.

From then on, no one interested in the issue trusted Charest when he talked about gun control. Much later, he was even forced to adopt a diametrically opposite position when he became leader of the Liberal Party of Quebec.

That's his cross to bear. As for me, I was finally able to put another check mark on my list of things to do.

23

"I have talked to women's groups [who say] this bill is so substantially important that if we yield or amend it in any way, they will be in jeopardy. I cannot discuss facts with them."

– Senator Raynell Andreychuck

His credibility now shot, Charest retreated from the issue. Yet that didn't keep the Conservative senators from carrying on without him they would never admit that they followed orders from the party leader anyway. Instead, they all covered their arguments with a social-democratic veneer, but despite their humanitarian pretensions, they always ended up with the same conclusion:

"I don't think the bill will help battered women," one of them told us during a meeting. "Nothing shows that registration will reduce domestic violence."

"Didn't you get material from the Provincial Association of Transition Houses of Saskatchewan?" Wendy asked. "How about the YMCA, whose position is endorsed by over a hundred and thirty women's organizations, many of which combat front-line violence . . ."

"Are you telling me how to do my job?" the senator inter-rupted. "I hope you're not questioning my judgment!"

Not all fifty-one Tory senators sounded like that – most were much more diplomatic. But the politicking was obvious: deep partisan trenches had been dug across the Senate floor. Instead of providing sober second thought, the Senate was replaying all the bickering that had occurred in the House.

Our opponents had the advantage, too. We had to fight our way through every obstruction we encountered. All they had to do was create new ones and delay, delay, delay.

As plain as their agenda was, we would have been hard-pressed to prove it was a conspiracy.

Or could we?

On August 23, 1995, we spotted the following message amongst the hundreds of lines that are posted every day on the gun lobby's electronic bulletin board:

On Monday night a local gun club hosted a meeting with three senators. . . . They said the best way to help them kill the bill was not by demanding that they defeat it but by presenting a list of no more than ten amendments that they could use. The plan was two-fold:
1. If they have amendments to discuss, they might hold on to the bill until Chrétien ends this session and the bill dies . . .
2. If it is amended and sent back to the Commons then it will die on the order paper.

We couldn't believe our eyes. They must have been

supremely confident – or extremely reckless – to post this on the Internet.

In any case, we now had verifiable data. We told one reporter, and he confirmed the quote by one of the senators. His article catalysed nationwide outrage:

AMENDMENTS WILL KILL BILL ON GUN CONTROL
    SENATORS SAY

TORY SENATORS STRATEGIZE TO KILL GUN LEGISLATION

TORY SENATORS USE GUN CONTROL FOR POLITICAL
    PURPOSES

TORY SENATORS PLOT GUN-BILL DEATH

TORY SENATORS ARE STALLING ON GUN BILL

SENATORS COULD PERMANENTLY STALL GUN LAW

PC SENATORS PLAY GUN-BILL ROULETTE

A PARTISAN SENATE DAMAGES PARLIAMENT

WHAT ARE THE SENATORS REALLY UP TO?

One letter to the editor in the Montreal *Gazette* appropriately summarized the backlash: "One of the reasons for having the Senate is to ensure that at least one level of government is invulnerable to the influence of special-interest groups whose objectives are detrimental to the general public. One cannot help but note the irony of our unelected Senate catering to the interests of gun owners, while our elected members of Parliament were able to stand up to their influence."

The senators scrambled to deny the reports. Pressed for comments, Conservative Senate Leader John Lynch-Staunton made sweeping declarations to the effect that the Upper House "should respect the will of the elected representatives."

As to whether his party would stall the bill, he added, "I don't think we want to do that."

Nice words. But when the hearings started, the Tory-dominated Senate committee chose to hear *more* testimonies than the House of Commons had called for in the spring. Most of the presentations would come from the same people and would consist of the same arguments.

Then the process was prolonged to accommodate even more witnesses: once the planned September hearings were completed, the committee would hear from additional individual experts every Wednesday of every week, until the end of November.

And *then* the committee's pro-gun senators decided to hold parallel consultations, to hear so-called concerned citizens in various cities (all of them in the West).

The toadying to gun interests was transparent. None of our supporters had asked for extended sessions. The senators who insisted on more hearings didn't even bother to attend most of the pro-control presentations. And when they did show up, they used the question period to make long-winded speeches against the bill – so much so that the chairman had to remind them they were supposed to question the witnesses, not lecture them.

We didn't have many options left.

Dear Senators,

Over the past two weeks, we have received several requests to identify potential witnesses who would support the gun-control bill in local hearings.

We are leaving it up to our supporters to decide whether they will testify. However, since the beginning of the Senate review, we have consistently expressed our opposition to cross-country hearings, and will not participate.

The arguments have already been made. Senators are now calling members of groups that have already testified to testify again. The Senate should be focussing on the substance of the arguments, not on how many times they hear them. These hearings contribute to the delays that are jeopardizing the bill.

Most of the senators organizing these hearings are on the record as opposing the legislation, and counselling the gun lobby on how to defeat the bill. In their correspondence and during the hearings in the capital, they challenge pro-control arguments but do not challenge pro-gun arguments. We do not believe anything supporters of the bill say will have an impact on these senators.

We do not wish to legitimize a process which seems primarily intended to placate the opponents of the legislation.

Pulling out of the hearings wasn't an easy decision. By refusing to engage in further consultations, we left the bill wide open to attacks.

But the opposite would have entailed an even greater risk. If we had taken part in the prolonged debates, we would have become accomplices in our own defeat.

To our relief, every last one of our supporters embraced the boycott. Police, doctors, lawyers, and community

activists all across the country turned down their invitation
to address the travelling Senate hearings.

It caught the senators off-guard; they didn't expected us to
walk away. They were so focussed on their manoeuvre to
delay, they hadn't thought that they might end up looking
biased and silly, presiding over a single-sided debate.

The rest of the committee, however, did realize that they
had to salvage a shred of integrity. Despite the pro-gun senators' griping over this "unseemly rush," the deadline was
moved up from November 30th to the 22nd.

It wasn't a big change – except that they could have kept
adding on more extensions otherwise. Putting an end to the
nonsense, *that* was a major victory.

                                 ❧

With tension mounting on a daily basis, so did the harass-
ment.

The message that was waiting for me when I got home
seemed innocuous at first: many people hesitate at length
when they chance upon an answering machine. There was
just a distant hum, like the echo in a big empty hall, with
barely audible whispers in the foreground. Then three shots
rang out in rapid succession, then three others, as loud as
they could be on the little speaker.

I didn't move, frozen in the middle of my apartment. The
low lighting I usually enjoy now seemed very dark, and for
the first time in my career as an activist, I wasn't so sure that
everything would be all right.

It wasn't the first threat Wendy and I had received. There had been other calls along the lines of, "The day Allan Rock and his goons come to my house is the day I'm coming over personally to settle this with you." But those were easy to attribute to some reckless yokel, especially if they lived too far away to represent an actual real danger.

The gunshots, however, were more evocative, raw, immediate. It took a twisted mind to inflict the sound of gunfire on a massacre survivor, and that only heightened the sense of peril.

Just as Wendy had, I passed the evidence on to the police, and was reassured to see how seriously they handled it. But as for abandoning the fight, the idea never entered my mind. We couldn't back down now, not at this point, not with so many people counting on us.

Nothing like this happened again, and I swiftly put it out of my mind.

⁂

We were in the last stretch.

As expected, the committee recommended a list of deadly amendments for the Senate to adopt, and even though the Liberals had now filled all the vacant seats, the Tories still had a majority of one. We also knew we couldn't count on a handful of adamantly anti-control Liberal senators, so we calculated that we needed to persuade no less than six Conservatives to reject the amendments.

Two of the victims' mothers, Suzanne Laplante-Edward and Thérèse Daviau, were so worried that they took it upon themselves to do some door-to-door campaigning in the Senate. It was as much against the rules as our own early attempts in the House had been, but who would have dared to set security guards on these women?

We also put together a travelling panel of experts. Every time we arranged a meeting with a senator, the panel would make an elaborate presentation right in that person's office. And since the Coalition now had eighteen thousand individual members, we decided to send them all a plea to flood the Senate in a tidal wave of support for the bill with calls, faxes, and letters.

But would it be enough?

It seemed like we couldn't even dent the objective façade put up by the point man who handled the dossier for the Conservatives, Senator Ron Ghitter. Poised and unflappable, he had been his colleagues' sole source of information about gun control until we showed up, and he always acted as if he were looking out for the country's best interests. He wouldn't be doing his job, he said, if he refrained from asking tough questions, but if they could be addressed to his satisfaction, he definitely wouldn't stand in the bill's way.

It was astonishing to see how many senators had not seen past his pro-gun arguments – some of them were honestly surprised to learn that sending the bill back to the House for "improvements" would endanger it!

We'd have had the hardest time convincing them he wasn't impartial . . . if he hadn't suddenly slipped:

"The firearms industry is worth more than $1 billion per year to the Canadian economy," he wrote to a group that had asked him to consider the price of guns to society. "The GST alone ought to cover the health-care costs you mention."

It was an incredibly callous statement to the hundreds of thousands who had lost – or had almost lost – a loved one to a bullet. It said that we, as a country, could afford to have people severely injured by gunshots if we made sure the gun industry pumped enough money into the economy.

The reactions were sharp and swift: "I wondered if Ghitter honestly believes that tax revenue – the economic benefits that firearms bring to our country – is what comes to the mind of a convenience-store worker when he has a handgun shoved in his face," wrote Ron Corbett, a columnist for the *Ottawa Sun*. "Who can say? Ghitter is boldly going where few have gone before. There are no reference points for this kind of logic."

The families affected by the Polytechnique massacre, now regrouped under the Fondation des victimes du 6 décembre contre la violence, were appalled by his remark. They organized one last press conference before the final vote, and made an impassioned last-ditch appeal to the other senators' decency.

Anne-Marie Edward's brother was one of the family members who spoke up that day. "I just want to make one comment," Jimmy said, his voice shaking with rage. "My sister received a bullet in mid-stomach. There was no need for taxes to 'cover the cost' of her injuries. She died from them.

"I hope the senator who made that remark is alone in his insensitivity. He's the one leading the charge to amend the bill, yet I believe that he does not represent most of his colleagues. I ask all senators to do the right thing. Do not let this piece of legislation die."

I can't add anything to that.

❧

On the evening of November 22, an unusual number of journalists set up camp in the Senate antechambers in anticipation of the vote. I had never seen such a circus before – you couldn't take a step without tripping over a cable or bumping into a commentator.

Inside, Wendy and I sat in the front row of the public gallery, just above the hundred-odd senators who had shown up. Dozens of our supporters were seated right behind us. The air crackled with rumours and electricity. As the senators mingled, just prior to the official proceedings, we eyed any huddle with mounting suspicion.

Such a group kept forming around Senator Gérald Beaudoin, the chair of the Senate Committee. His aide had confided to me a few days earlier that it *might* be possible to convince him to abstain from voting on his committee's recommendations.

We figured we should give it a try.

Since Senator Beaudoin was a professor of law, our friend Louise got her acquaintances in the legal profession, many of whom were his former students, to call him. And, after standing guard in the parliamentary cafeteria, Suzanne even managed to corner him in person.

"You know who I am and why I'm here," she told him

point-blank. "You also know what your party is trying to do. You're not going to be part of this scandal, are you?"

He was kind to her and didn't deny the dirty tricks that had occurred over the course of the hearings. But he didn't promise anything either. We had no idea what his final position would be.

The rumour that he might abstain had spread, and members of both parties kept hounding him to "do his duty," whatever that may have been. But no matter how hard they pushed, he just nodded and smiled, and gestured them to calm down whenever they got too assertive.

I watched him closely as he took his seat. A small, quiet man with sparse white hair, he didn't fit my image of a powerful player, yet his attitude spoke volumes about the strength of his character: his expression playful behind his thick glasses, he acted as though the world was a bed of roses, and we were all his grandchildren – a little unruly but never enough to try his patience. He didn't let anybody get under his skin.

The bell signalling the start of the vote stopped ringing, and the conversations died down.

The first order of business was a private amendment to the bill, which took another stab at decriminalizing the failure to register. Such lone motions tend to be summarily rejected, but in this particular instance, all bets were off. Opponents of the bill did not care *which* amendments were being discussed, or *who* had submitted them. They only needed *one* to go through, and the bill would be sent back to die in the House.

The speaker took the floor.

"All those in favour of the motion will please say Yea."

"YEA."

"All those opposed will please say Nay."

"NAY."

There was hardly any difference!

I was terrified – I hadn't expected *this* vote to be so close.

A formal head count would have to be taken. One by one, the senators who favoured the amendment rose to let the clerk register their names.

My spirits plummeted when I saw that people we had counted on were reneging on their promises and were now backing the amendment. The rare Conservatives who still sided with us were as surprised as we were: they looked up, apologetically, and one of them mimed a silent tear.

The tallying took about five minutes, yet it seemed much longer than that. We tried to count the senators ourselves, but they weren't all visible from our seats, and we lost track after the first two dozen.

"In favour: 41. Against: 57. Abstention: 1. The amendment is rejected."

We let out our breath, but our relief didn't last long. All the other amendments would now be put to the vote as a single package. And unlike the first proposition, this set bore the stamp of the Senate Standing Committee on Legal and Constitutional Affairs. It had been drafted after nine weeks of thorough review and seemed so perfectly legitimate.

If a single senator's motion had garnered 41 votes, then these proposals would surely land more support.

"All those in favour of the motion will please say Yea," continued the speaker.

Again, from the spoken yeas and nays it was impossible to discern a majority, so we went through another registered vote. And when we saw that more people were rising to support this package of amendments, we thought we had lost the fight.

Then we noticed that Senator Beaudoin remained seated, allowing the wave of yea-sayers swoosh past him. He stood only up when the nays were registered, becoming the first Conservative to *reject* the amendments.

Puzzled murmurs spread through the Red Chamber. If the man who submitted the report did not believe in it, how could anyone else do so in good conscience?

Should a few principled senators have intended to abstain, Beaudoin's vote may have convinced them to cast their ballots *against* the amendments instead. But until the count was in, we couldn't be sure. We weren't able to think anyway – we both had tears in our eyes, and all Wendy and I kept asking ourselves was, *Are we going to make it? Please, please, please, are we going to make it?*

❧

Suzanne

When we were called in to identify Anne-Marie's body on the night of the massacre, the officer told us how lucky we were.

That's the word he used – lucky. Jim and I gave him the long stare, but we soon understood what he had meant. Unlike some of the other girls, our daughter had not been shot in the face. None of her wounds were visible, and I was immensely grateful for that.

"She's already left us," my son Jimmy said. "This is not her. Anne-Marie always smiles."

I made my way around the table where she lay, lifeless. I caressed the nape of her neck, slowly turned her head towards me, and kissed her forehead.

"Goodbye, Anne-Marie. I love you."

Then a singular thing happened. I felt a power surge, transferred from her body to my own – as if her unspent energy had been passed on to me. And I heard her voice scream, "This is all I can give you. For God's sake, Mom, DO SOMETHING WITH IT."

For God's sake, Mom, do something with it. The words were still ringing in my ears as the vote was tallied.

I was sitting white-knuckled in the press gallery, just behind Heidi and Wendy. We all tried to put up a brave front, but we had worked so hard to get to where we were, it was unbearable to think that everything could collapse at the last moment.

My hands and feet were frozen in terror. Warm tears were flowing down my cheeks.

This is it, Anne-Marie, this is what we did on your behalf. It's now out of our hands, so help us if you can.

It was a close call. On that fateful day, forty-six senators voted to amend the bill and send it to its death.

But fifty-three others chose to keep it as is.

24

"Finally, a fitting memorial to the fourteen victims of the massacre."

– Editorial, Montreal *Gazette*

I'm taking a leisurely stroll in downtown Ottawa. A gentle snow has been falling all night, and the capital is dressed in holiday whites. It feels like a new country.

It is.

Cheerfully adorned with festive decorations, the boutiques and restaurants only add to the celebratory feeling. In spite of the snow, the small newspaper kiosk on Sparks Street has placed its selection of dailies on an outside stand to attract customers, and I can't help stopping to glance proudly at the banner headlines about the passage of the bill. *We've made history*, I think for the hundredth time.

The articles call it an easy win, a breeze, a "no-show at Senate corral." Once the amendments were rejected, few senators dared to oppose the legislation. In the very final vote, the untouched bill was adopted by sixty-four to twenty-eight against – a count that too easily concealed the colossal tug-of-war behind it all. Few people seem to realize that if only four senators had voted differently in the previous round, we would not have anything to celebrate today.

I don't care. Everything that weighed on my shoulders in the last six years has just vanished. There's no crisis, no appointment, nothing at all on my "to do" list. For the last eighteen hours, all I've been doing is partying, sleeping, and yelling "We did it," over and over.

The congratulations haven't stopped pouring in from friends, the victims' families, even the media, and I have such a delirious grin on my face that the people I'm passing are turning to stare. *Do you feel the change in the air? Do you realize how this will affect us all?*

The future is now wide open, and the feeling is indescribable. Everything seems possible, as long as I put my mind to it. My other worries have all been eclipsed, my uncertainties, swept away. I'm finally at peace.

I know there's more to come. The law won't be proclaimed for twelve more days, and given how much leeway the act gives gun owners to register, it will take eight years before it comes into full force. During that period, the gun lobby will fight it every step of the way.

We'll keep an eye out for it. But as of December 6 this year, the country will be a better place to live.

And boy, does it ever feel good to have been a part of that.

AFTERWORD

by Wendy Cukier

When he joined us at the party celebrating the passage of the legislation, Justice Minister Allan Rock concluded his toast, "We have finished Phase One. Now, it's onto Phase Two."

We all laughed. Exhausted and drained, I thought we had made our contribution and could get back to our lives. I had no inkling that we would have to spend at least as much time protecting our gains.

As I write this, it's been four years since the bill became law. We surmounted several hurdles, but many others remain.

A quick overview:

• It took six months before the regulations were tabled. And when they were, the opposition was so strong that the proposals were hastily withdrawn. They weren't finalized until two years later.

The quantity of details was mind-boggling. A mere error in wording almost made us lose the controls over handguns that were already in place (the mistake was corrected at the eleventh hour). Overall, we wrote more briefs and testified before more committees than we had during the struggle for the bill.

• During the same period, the start-up date for gun registration was delayed no less than four times. It's a good thing the final deadline was enshrined in the legislation – otherwise, we may never have seen a single rifle registered.

• Our resolve was fuelled by a series of horrific events throughout the world:

In Scotland, 16 schoolchildren and their teacher were murdered by a gun-club member, who then killed himself. (Within six months, Great Britain banned 90 percent of handguns, after which a new government banned the remainder.)

In Tasmania, 35 people were killed and 18 injured by a gun collector armed with semi-automatic rifles. (Australia then improved its gun law to include national licensing and registration, as well as a buy-back of semi-automatic weapons.)

And in the United States, school shootings took on a tragic familiarity. In a little over a year, 11 people were killed and 20 wounded in no less than five different massacres – yet this wasn't enough for the government to tighten gun control. Only after two youths murdered 13 people and wounded 23 in Colorado did the government envision taking modest legislative action.

• Four years after its massive demonstration on Parliament Hill, the gun lobby held a new rally, inviting guest speakers to argue that massacres take place *because* the victims are unarmed, and to liken gun control to the "cultural war" waged by blacks, feminists, and homosexuals. We had no trouble refuting these arguments, but it did show that the fight was getting uglier.

• A new federal election came and went in 1997. Out of five parties, the Reform Party and the Conservatives pledged to repeal the law, while the NDP sat firmly on the fence.

A number of gun-lobby members also ran for office, and the head of the National Firearms Association openly asked his peers in the U.S. to donate money to his organization so that he could funnel it to the appropriate candidates. The initiative clearly violated the spirit of the laws against political campaigns funded by foreign interests.

The Liberal Party, which had introduced the gun law, was returned to power with a strong majority, but the position of its adversaries on gun control remained unchanged.

• Four provinces, two territories, and two gun groups (lead by the government of Alberta) challenged the law before the Alberta Court of Appeal. The Coalition intervened in support of the government, lined up witnesses, drafted dozens of documents, briefed the media and tried not to scream upon hearing the half-baked arguments presented against the law. ("Millions of dollars' worth of jewels are stolen every year and we do not force owners to register them, do we?" As if diamond rings ever killed anyone!)

Our lawyers donated a considerable amount of time, but the legal bill still came to more than $100,000. No easy amount for a grassroots organization to raise, particularly when fighting provincial governments that have unlimited access to taxpayers' money.

The judges ruled 3 to 2 in our favour, and the Chief Justice unequivocally stated that licensing and registration were "a small price to pay for the privilege of being allowed to possess and use a dangerous weapon." It was music to our ears, but a short-lived victory. The ruling is currently being appealed to the Supreme Court.

ॐ

Other developments were more positive. When the government of France announced that it would introduce more controls, it specifically credited our work as its inspiration. Meanwhile, a UN resolution sponsored by thirty-three countries called on all nations to adopt registration, licensing, and storage regulations. And on the home front, numerous inquests have recommended that our law be fully implemented as quickly as possible.

In some ways, we are victims of our success. Since most people think the battle has ended, it's increasingly difficult to muster support. And we're not just fighting gun lobbyists any more, but government bureaucrats who want to get the implementation process out of the way quickly, no matter the compromises to public safety.

While the Coalition is still putting up a strong defence, we are all tired. The fight should not have taken this long, and the lesson is that it won't be over soon.

If Phase Two ever ends, it will just herald the beginning of Phase Three.

APPENDIX

For their outstanding contributions to society, Heidi Rathjen and Wendy Cukier have received the following recognition:

- Honorary Doctorate, Faculty of Law, Concordia University
- Honorary Doctorate, Faculty of Medicine, Laval University
- Special Tribute, École Polytechnique
- Special Mention, Canadian Association of Chiefs of Police
- Certificate of Merit, Canadian Public Health Association
- Civilian Commendation, Ottawa Police Services Board
- Women of Distinction, YWCA of Montreal and Toronto
- Women of the Year Award, Jewish Women International (Toronto)
- World Congress on Violence on Human Coexistence Award, International Association for Scientific Exchange on Violence and Human Coexistence

Heidi Rathjen was named one of *La Presse*'s Personalities of the Week, the *Gazette*'s Women to Watch, *Hour Magazine*'s Young Turks and *Maclean's* 100 Canadians to Watch. She also won the Quebec Justice Award. She's now the strategist of the Quebec Coalition for Tobacco Control (for which she got another major law passed), and remains the volunteer vice-president of the Coalition for Gun Control.

Wendy Cukier received a Canada 125 medal, the *Toronto Sun*'s Woman on the Move Award and, in association with Strategic Communications, the Canadian Direct Marketing Association's Silver Medal. Ryersonian of the year, she still teaches Administration and Information Management and remains the volunteer president of the Coalition for Gun Control.

A portion of the revenues generated by this book is being donated to the Coalition for Gun Control.

To make a donation of your own, or to get more information about the Coalition's current activities, please write to:

Coalition for Gun Control
Box 395, Station D
Toronto, ON M6P 3J9
fax: (416) 604-0209
e-mail: 71417.763@compuserve.com
http://www.kipawa.com/guncontrol

Coalition pour le contrôle des armes
1301 Sherbrooke Street East
Montreal, QC H2L 1M3
fax: (514) 528-2598
e-mail: 104360.1426@compuserve.com